BATTERED WOMEN, CHILDREN, AND WELFARE REFORM

Sage Series on Violence Against Women

Series Editors

Claire M. Renzetti
St. Joseph's University

Jeffrey L. Edleson
University of Minnesota

In this series . . .

BATTERED WOMEN, CHILDREN, AND WELFARE REFORM

The Ties That Bind

Ruth A. Brandwein
Editor

Sage Series on Violence Against Women

SAGE Publications
International Educational and Professional Publisher
Thousand Oaks   London   New Delhi

For information:

SAGE Publications, Inc.
2455 Teller Road
Thousand Oaks, California 91320
E-mail: order@sagepub.com

SAGE Publications Ltd.
6 Bonhill Street
London EC2A 4PU
United Kingdom

SAGE Publications India Pvt. Ltd.
M-32 Market
Greater Kailash I
New Delhi 110 048 India

Printed in the United States of America

Library of Congress Cataloging-in-Publication Data

Main entry under title:

Battered women, children, and welfare reform: The ties that bind/
    by Ruth A. Brandwein, editor
        p.   cm.—(Sage series on violence against women; v. 11)
    Includes bibliographical references and index.
    ISBN 0-7619-1148-0 (cloth: alk. paper)
    ISBN 0-7619-1149-9 (pbk.: alk. paper)
    1. Abused women—Government policy—United States.
    2. Abused women—United States—Economic conditions.
    3. Welfare recipients—Abuse of—United States. 4. Public
    welfare—United States. 5. Family violence—United States.
    I. Brandwein, Ruth A.   II. Series.
    HV1445 .B37 1998
    362.82′9256′0973—ddc21   98-40067

This book is printed on acid-free paper.

99 00 01 02 03 10 9 8 7 6 5   4 3 2

Acquiring Editor:	C. Terry Hendrix
Production Editor:	Sherrise M. Roehr
Production Assistant:	Karen Wiley
Typesetter/Designer:	Marion Warren

For my parents, Kate and the late Charles Solin,
who taught me to fight for justice for all, and for my children,
Lorena Epstein and Garth Brandwein,
who taught me to love and care for my own.

Contents

Acknowledgments

I am grateful to many people for making this book possible. First, I thank Dean Kay Dea and the Belle Spafford Committee for selecting me to occupy the Endowed Spafford Chair at the University of Utah Graduate School of Social Work, where the work for this book was begun. I especially thank Anissa Rogers, my research assistant; and Amy Hallissey, my secretary at the school for their competence and unfailing good humor. Anissa did much of the collecting and inputting of data on which Chapter 4 is based. All members of my advisory council were most helpful, but special thanks go to Salt Lake City Police Chief Ruben Ortega; Mary Noonan, then Director of Utah's Office of Children and Families; and Robin Arnold-Williams, then Deputy Director of Utah's Department of Human Services for giving me permission to access their data. Thanks also go to Deeda Seed, then director of JEDI Women, for encouraging me to examine the links between family violence and welfare.

At the School of Social Welfare at the State University of New York at Stony Brook, I offer my appreciation to Diana Filiano, who served as my research assistant and helped in so many ways. I also must thank Dean Frances Brisbane for her ongoing support, and my secretary Margaret O'Neill for all her efforts. My very special gratitude goes to Florence Graziano, administrative assistant at the school's Child Welfare Training Project, whose patience, cooperation, and knowledge of computer software made the final manuscript a quality job rather than a horror, and to Orlando Capalong at Information Systems in the Health Sciences Center Library for solving the mysteries of incompatible disks.

I also express my gratitude to C. Terry Hendrix and Claire Renzetti at Sage for their support and encouragement of this project. Finally, these acknowledgments would not be complete without a very special thanks to Garry Greenbowe, who helped keep me sane through this entire process.

Foreword

During the 1990s, Congress enacted two major policy innovations affecting women: the Violence Against Women Act of 1994, and the Personal Responsibility and Work Opportunity Act of 1996. The Violence Against Women Act broke new ground when it was enacted by establishing federal remedies and safeguards for victims of family violence. The Personal Responsibility Act (PRA) also broke new ground, by repealing the Aid to Families with Dependent Children program which had provided financial assistance to single mothers and their children since 1935. The PRA replaced AFDC with the Temporary Assistance to Needy Families program (TANF), which requires recipients to work outside the home and imposes lifetime time limits on welfare eligibility.

The new welfare law has enormous implications for the safety of women and children who have experienced family violence. Studies show that women often use welfare to flee domestic violence and that domestic violence sometimes prevents them from moving into paid employment. Congress included a provision in the PRA to attenuate the impact of welfare reform on domestic violence victims when it passed the Family Violence Option. However, Congress left it up to each state to decide whether to adopt the provision.

This important collection of essays is the first to examine welfare and domestic violence together, as the interrelated issues that they are. It provides essential empirical research and rich scholarly analyses that examine the nexus between family violence and the need for welfare. Importantly, the book takes a broad view of family violence and considers how child abuse, as well as wife battering, interacts with the need for welfare.

Each chapter is written by an expert in her field. Readers may want to dip into the volume to read about particular issues: for example, Roberts' legal analysis of the complexities of pursuing child support from an abusive father, or Raphael's anecdotes about how domestic violence victims are prevented from leaving welfare. Others may want to explore Brandwein's findings about the related timing of welfare use and reports of domestic violence incidents, or Boyer's discussion of the links among child sexual abuse, adolescent pregnancy, and the subsequent need for welfare. All readers will be moved by the vivid first person accounts of women who have survived abuse and relied on welfare. They also should find illuminating Brandwein's concluding consideration of the pitfalls of current federal policies.

One of the failings of contemporary debates about welfare is that the policy is typically framed as though women and gender are not involved. *Battered Women, Children, and Welfare Reform* brings visibility to the women who are the subjects of welfare law, and does so from feminist perspectives. Integrative and interdisciplinary, this valuable collection worries about the impact of policies on women. It should be required reading for students, women's advocates, service providers—and for my colleagues in Congress.

THE HONORABLE PATSY T. MINK
Congresswoman from Hawaii

PART I

INTRODUCTION

1

Family Violence, Women, and Welfare

Ruth A. Brandwein

Domestic policy has once again captured the spotlight on the national stage. In the last few years, two major and sometimes contradictory areas of domestic policy—family violence and public welfare—have been the focus of intense public debate and national legislation.

One out of every two women in the United States will experience abuse at least once during her marriage, one out of four will experience it on a recurring basis, and the National Crime Survey has estimated that more than two million women are battered annually (Langan & Innes, 1986; Russell, 1990; Walker, 1984). Every year, millions of women call their local battered women's hotlines and thousands are housed in shelters. In one state alone in 1996, domestic violence programs provided services to more than 100,000 victims, and battered women's shelters housed more than 11,000 women and their children (Pennsylvania Coalition Against Domestic Violence, 1997).

The Violence Against Women Act, passed by Congress in 1994, was the culmination of years of effort by the battered women's movement to educate the public and lawmakers about the plight and needs of abused women. This law epitomizes a major change in public awareness and understanding of the phenomenon of domestic abuse. Rather than blaming the victims of such violence, it signals the public's support and sympathy for the victims. Although much remains to be done, federal, state, and local governments are moving to provide needed services to victims and to punish their abusers. Overwhelmingly, victims of domestic violence are women, so it is especially significant that the act recognizes the gender issue by specifically addressing violence against *women*.

Simultaneously, the other major domestic issue that has captured the public's attention has been public welfare, culminating in the passage of the Personal Responsibility and Work Opportunity Reconciliation Act of 1996 (PRA; National Association for Social Workers, 1996) by Congress. This law embodies a sea change in how U.S. society treats families in need.

In 1997, 10 million women and their children were receiving public assistance in the United States (U.S. Department of Health and Human Services [DHHS], 1997). This number has been rapidly dwindling because of the recent changes in federal and state laws. The PRA eliminates Aid to Families With Dependent Children (AFDC), a 60-year-old safety net program that had entitled poor mothers and their children to financial assistance on the basis of need, for as long as the need continued, until the youngest child reached age 18.

The new law replaces that program with a time-limited Block Grant, Temporary Assistance to Needy Families (TANF). This is essentially a funding stream to the states to run their own state programs of aid. The federal law, however, does put conditions on states for the receipt of these funds. Among the most draconian of these requirements are arbitrary time limits on the receipt of aid: a 5-year lifetime limit for aid, regardless of need; a 2-year limit for finding full-time employment; and a requirement to be involved in a work experience program of 20 to 35 hours per week within 2 months of initial receipt of aid. It also requires mothers of infants as young as 3 months to work outside the home, prohibits aid to most immigrants,[1] and allows the entire family to be cut from assistance, rather than just withholding the mother's portion, if the mother does not comply with work regulations. It allows states to set up residency requirements that would create different levels of assistance or waiting periods for women moving from another state; family caps that prohibit additional aid for any children born while the mother is on welfare; and other punitive restrictions.

The rhetoric preceding and accompanying passage of this legislation was that these women are not deserving of public support, that such support creates dependency, and that they could provide for themselves and their children if only government did not assist them for too long (Gilder, 1981; Mead, 1986, 1992; Payne, 1996). The image of welfare in U.S. society conjures up stereotypes of lazy, shiftless women who prefer to lounge at home drinking beer, watching television, and procreating. The often unspoken message, supported by sensational media stories, is that these welfare recipients are primarily young, unmarried black women with large broods of children. The facts are that more welfare recipients are white, that they have an average of slightly fewer than two children per family, and that most leave the rolls after 2 years. It is easier, however, to enact punitive legislation when those targeted are considered the "other." If they appear to be different from "us," we are less likely to sympathize with them and they can be more easily marginalized, stigmatized, and treated punitively.

The genius of the battered women's movement is that it has successfully conveyed the message that domestic violence cuts across all groups—white as well as Hispanic and African American, and middle class as well as poor. The Nicole Brown Simpson case conveyed the message that even celebrities, even wealthy, privileged women, were not immune from abusive spouses. When a problem is recognized as affecting all of *us*, rather than just *them*, it is more amenable to public policy leading to positive change. This is evident in the Violence Against Women legislation and the thousands of programs in communities throughout the nation that have begun to invest public funds to address the problem of domestic abuse.

Ironically, often the same women are targeted in both sets of legislation: the Violence Against Women Act and the Personal Responsibility Act. When observed through the lens of domestic violence, the women are victims in need of assistance. When observed through the lens of public welfare, many of these same women are demonized and assistance is denied or provided sparingly and with punitive conditions. Although it is certainly true that not all women who are abused are welfare recipients and that not all welfare recipients have been abused, growing evidence suggests that the two issues are inextricably linked. This linkage was recognized by Senators Paul Wellstone (D, Minnesota) and Patti Murray (D, Washington), who sponsored a Family Violence Amendment to the federal Personal Responsibility Act. Included in the final bill as an option that states can choose to adopt, the amendment calls for the confidential screening of applicants and recipients of public assistance to determine whether they have been victims of domestic violence. Assessments are then to be undertaken to determine what services are needed and whether waivers from some or all requirements for receiving aid are necessary in order to prevent further jeopardy or victimization of the individual woman. As of this writing, 28 states have chosen this option and are in the beginning stages of implementation (NOW Legal Defense and Education Fund, 1997).

How is the use of welfare linked with family violence? How does a woman get to the point of needing public assistance? What keeps her from getting off welfare? This book explores the links between the experience of family violence and the use of public welfare, two phenomena that are usually studied separately.

The contributors intentionally employ the term *family violence,* rather than *domestic violence,* although these terms are sometimes used interchangeably. *Domestic violence* is used to denote spousal or other intimate partner abuse, whereas *family violence,* the more generic term, is employed to include not only partner abuse but also other abuse within the family. In this book, we also explore how child abuse, another form of family violence, may be linked with the need for public assistance.

Links Between Family Violence and Welfare

The origins of this book can be traced to the fall of 1995. I was about to take up residency as the Spafford Chair in Women and Family Issues at the University of Utah School of Social Work. Earlier, when negotiating my anticipated activities and work plan with the dean, I had told him that my two areas of interest were family violence and women in poverty. Because another visiting scholar had recently addressed the issue of women in poverty in Utah, we agreed that during my 6-month residency I would focus on the issue of family violence.

By late 1995, however, the welfare issue was coming to a boil in Washington. Because of my concerns for poor women, I had been actively advocating against many of the proposed welfare bills then being considered in Congress. How was I to walk away from this historic struggle for 6 months? Yet, I had made a commitment to work on the issue of family violence while in Utah, which, up to then, had been largely ignored as a problem in the state. I could not divide what little time I had to work on two separate issues. As I pondered this dilemma, I had what used to be known in feminist circles as a "click" experience. It suddenly came to me that I could work on both together because they were related. Rather than divide my time, exploring the connection between the two would provide a more synergistic approach to both issues. The question was, *How* were they related? How does this relationship between family violence and the need for welfare manifest itself?

Financial Support Enables Woman to Leave Abuser

The most obvious link is that when a woman is in an abusive relationship, one reason why she cannot leave is that she is financially dependent on her abuser. Welfare, though paltry at best, has offered an option—a lifeline for some women. One clear link, then, is that welfare is used by women to escape from abusive situations.

Simultaneously with my musings, several researchers were beginning to document the frequency of current or former domestic violence in the lives of welfare recipients. These studies are referred to in subsequent chapters.

Abuser Sabotages Woman's Attempts
to Work and Leave Welfare

Abuse not only may drive a woman to use welfare but also may keep her poor and on welfare. A second link is that of women in welfare-to-work programs who are obstructed from education, training, and jobs by abusive spouses (Raphael, 1995). Many women try to prepare themselves for employment but are hindered by partners who are jealous or insecure or who fear losing control in the relationship if their partners become economically independent.

Long-Term Effects of Abuse May Create
Continuing Need for Welfare

The long-term effects of abuse may be another link between abuse and welfare. About half the women who apply for public assistance leave the rolls within 1 to 2 years (Ellwood, 1988). Nevertheless, many return, and others are long-term recipients. Why do they stay? Some politicians and conservative commentators believe that these women are caught in a cycle of dependency. Mounting evidence, however, suggests that at least some of those remaining on assistance have been so emotionally or even physically damaged by their abuse experiences that they are unable to seek or keep jobs. The long-term effects of abuse that keep women on welfare have not been sufficiently recognized.

Welfare Child Support Reporting
Requirements Can Add Risk of Abuse

Another area of linkage between family violence and welfare is not a causative one, but a recognition of increased danger and risk of family violence for welfare recipients. To receive public assistance, applicants are required to provide information about the paternity of their children and the whereabouts of the fathers. This information is required so that the state can attempt to collect child support payments and recoup state expenditures for welfare payments. Such attempts, however, may create a double bind for victims of abuse. Providing information about a child's father may further endanger an already abused woman, but not providing the information may put her at risk of being denied the financial support she and her children desperately need.

Prior Child Sexual Abuse May Lead to Need for Welfare

As I continued to ponder possible links between these two phenomena, I came on several more speculative connections. What, I wondered, were the links between child abuse and welfare? It is recognized that child sexual abuse can result in long-term consequences, including low self-esteem, sexual acting out, and post-traumatic stress disorder (American Psychological Association, 1994; Beitchman et al., 1992). How many women on welfare may have been abused as children? Girls who have been sexually abused may become promiscuous. If so, they are more likely than others to become pregnant at a young age (Musick, 1993). Although only a small proportion (8%) of the welfare population at any time are unwed teenage mothers, a large proportion of women on welfare had their first children as teenagers.

To what extent might that earlier child abuse have led to teenage pregnancy and subsequent use of welfare? If policymakers and the public understood that childhood sexual abuse may be a significant factor in teenage pregnancy, perhaps the punitive rhetoric surrounding unwed teen motherhood might abate. Prevention of such abuse—or, when it cannot be prevented, timely therapeutic intervention with its victims—might have a more salutary effect in preventing subsequent teenage pregnancy and the possible need for public welfare than all the calls for abstinence and punitive legislation.

Current Child Abuse May Lead to Need for Welfare

Current child abuse might also be linked with the use of welfare. In over half the cases that involve partner abuse, child abuse is also present (Bowker, Arbitell, & Ferron, 1988; Stark & Flitcraft, 1985). Often, the abuser is abusing both his wife and his children. In a typical situation, in which the perpetrator is the father, stepfather, or live-in boyfriend, the mother who is not the abuser but who herself may be abused is still held responsible for the protection of the child. The law defines "failure to protect" as a valid reason for removing a child from the home.

In such a situation, the mother has two options: She can leave, or she can force the man to leave. In either case, if he has been providing financial support, she is left in economic jeopardy. If she does neither, she risks the real possibility of losing custody of her child because of "failure to protect." If she does leave, she may become homeless and need welfare to support herself and her child or children. If she is successful in making the abuser leave the home, it is unlikely that he will continue to provide financial support. If she is able to find a job, she may find herself in a Catch-22 situation: She is not at home supervising the child and may be deemed neglectful; and her lack of direct supervision of the abused child can be considered "failure to protect" by the local child protective services agency. If she cannot find a job or if she decides that she must remain at home to properly supervise the child, she may be forced to turn to public welfare for support.

Summary of Links Between Family Violence and Welfare

There are, then, at least six areas of linkage between family violence and the use of welfare:

1. A woman may go on welfare to be financially able to leave her abuser.
2. A woman may be unable to leave welfare because her abuser is sabotaging her attempts to pursue education, training, or employment.
3. A woman may find it difficult to work or prepare herself for a job because of the long-term effects of abuse.
4. The abused woman seeking welfare may be further endangered by child support enforcement requirements.
5. A woman who was a victim of earlier child sexual abuse may be more vulnerable to early pregnancy and the ensuing need for public assistance.
6. A mother whose child has been abused by the male provider may need to seek welfare assistance in order to provide full-time supervision.

Family Violence and Welfare: Cause or Effect?

Acknowledging the links between welfare and family violence holds some strategic dangers. Some will conclude, as did Senator Dole at the 1996 Republican Convention, that welfare *causes* abuse, rather than the reverse. This conclusion appears to confirm the conservative mantra of how harmful welfare is. Recognizing the links between the two can reinforce the notion that those on welfare are different from the rest of us: It is *those people* who are so violent. This notion can lead to further stigmatization and marginalization of welfare recipients. It may also undo the productive efforts of the battered women's movement to educate the public about the universal nature of family violence. If, however, it can be documented that the violence leads to the need for welfare, rather than the use of welfare leading to violence, the public and policymakers may change their perception of who the welfare client is.

If any of *us* might be victims of family violence and might then need to receive public assistance, the negative stereotyping of welfare recipients may be lessened. It is important, therefore, to learn not only of the frequency of abuse among welfare recipients but also of the causal connections between them.

It is necessary not only to demonstrate a frequency between family violence and the use of welfare but also to determine which came first or how closely the two events are related in time. Unless this is done, the mistaken notion that welfare, or "broken families," or "those people" who "choose" to be on welfare causes family violence will not be dispelled. If women apply for welfare soon after a violent incident, one can be more confident that the violence caused the need for welfare, rather than the reverse. The closer the temporal connection between the two, the more likely the violence triggered the use of welfare.

Description of the Book

Countless volumes have been written about family violence. Similarly, many works have analyzed the welfare system. Most books on family violence, however, focus on causation and intervention with victims but not on policy, whereas most books on welfare policy tend to ignore its effect on individuals. This is the first book to examine the connections between family violence and broad policy questions linking policy implementation with its impact on real people. This volume provides a comprehensive introduction and overview of how the use of public assistance is related to family violence; thus, it affords a unique contribution to the current state of knowledge in the field.

This book is designed for a multidisciplinary audience. It will be useful to practitioners, faculty, and students in the fields of women's studies, marriage and family counseling, social work, psychology, pastoral counseling, sociology, public administration, public policy, and criminal justice and law. Although based on fully referenced scholarship, it is my aim as its editor to make this book accessible to policymakers, practitioners, students, and an informed lay audience, as well as scholars. Therefore, the contributors have attempted to make it readable and interesting by generous use of case material to leaven the academic research cited.

The volume bridges several disciplines and policy areas usually considered separately. The authors of individual chapters represent several of these disciplines, but in addition one chapter combines personal reflections, written by survivors of family violence who are current or past recipients of welfare. It is essential to learn not only from experts but also from those who have direct experience with the phenomena under study.

The only chapter in Part I, Chapter 1, addresses the links between partner abuse and welfare. In Part II, the two chapters following this one review the current literature in the field and provide examples of how abuse makes and keeps women poor and financially vulnerable. Chapter 2, by Martha Davis, explores the question, How does partner abuse create the need for welfare? She examines poverty and the economic pressures facing battered women. Chapter 3, by Jody Raphael, explores how continuing domestic violence keeps women poor and prevents them from leaving welfare. She provides data and case material from around the nation, illustrating how abusers undermine women's efforts to become financially independent. She discusses both immediate obstacles to leaving welfare created by abusers, as well as impediments related to the long-term effects of abuse.

In Chapter 4, I summarize my own research that demonstrates how application for welfare is closely linked in time with domestic violence incidents. Illustrations from focus groups amplify the quantitative data reported.

Chapter 5, by attorney Paula Roberts, provides a thorough and comprehensive review of the child support features of the new federal law and how they will affect survivors of domestic violence. She offers suggestions for how the legislation should be operationalized to minimize potential danger to women and their children.

Chapter 6, by Diane Stuart, an administrator of domestic violence programs for the state of Utah and a former director of a battered women's shelter, provides firsthand examples of the links between violence and welfare, as well as suggestions for policy and practice.

The last chapter in Part II, Chapter 7, is a compilation of firsthand experiences by three women who are survivors of family violence and who have also had to use the welfare system. They recount their ordeals with abusers and their experiences with the welfare system. For all its limitations, welfare offered a lifeline when they needed it. The implications of welfare "reform," which may limit welfare's future availability to women in need, is frightening. Their first-person accounts help humanize the issue. When developing policies, preparing budgets, and implementing programs, it is vital to remember that these will affect real people, each with his or her own life struggles.

Part III of the book comprises three chapters pertaining to child abuse and the use of welfare. Chapter 8, by Diana Pearce, sets out the issue of mother-blaming in relation to child abuse, the economic situation facing mothers who must protect their children from further abuse, and the implications for welfare use. This is illustrated in my Chapter 9, using data and case material based on a speech by a state official responsible for child protective services. In Chapter 10, Debra Boyer furnishes a background and reports on her original research concerning the relationship among child sexual abuse, teenage pregnancy, and implications for subsequent use of welfare.

In Part IV, in the final chapter, I summarize what is known in the field, discuss the policy implications of current welfare legislation and the possible effects on survivors of abuse, and offer recommendations for alternative short- and long-term policies and programs.

It is my hope that this book will contribute to the dialogue on public policy concerning the plight of abused and poor women. If it can help infuse in that debate the reality and humanity of women's lives, perhaps it can lead to more enlightened policies affecting those in need.

Note

1. This was modified in 1997 legislation, mainly for elderly and disabled immigrants.

References

American Psychological Association. (1994). *Desk reference to the diagnostic criteria from DSM-IV* (4th ed.). Washington, DC: Author.

Beitchman, J., et al. (1992). A review of the long-term effects of child sexual abuse. *Journal of Child Abuse and Neglect, 16,* 110-118.

Bowker, L., Arbitell, M., & Ferron, J. (1988). On the relationship between wife beating and child abuse. In K. Yllo & M. Bograd (Eds.), *Feminist perspectives on wife abuse* (pp. 153-174). Newbury Park, CA: Sage.

Ellwood, D. (1988). *Poor support: Poverty in the American family.* New York: Basic Books.

Gilder, G. (1981). *Wealth and poverty.* New York: Basic Books.

Langan, K. E., & Innes, C. A. (1986). *Preventing domestic violence against women* (Bureau of Justice Statistics special report). Washington, DC: U.S. Department of Justice.

Mead, L. (1986). *Beyond entitlement: The social obligations of citizenship.* New York: Free Press.

Mead, L. (1992). *The new politics of poverty: The nonworking poor in America*. New York: Basic Books.

Musick, J. (1993). *Poor, young, and pregnant: The psychology of teenage motherhood*. New Haven, CT: Yale University Press.

National Association for Social Workers. (1996, August 27). *Personal Responsibility and Work Opportunity Reconciliation Act of 1996 (H.R. 37334) and Public Law 104-93: Summary of provisions*.

NOW Legal Defense and Education Fund. (1997, September). *Summary of state activity regarding family violence provisions in their state welfare plans*. Washington DC: Author.

Payne, J. (1996, November-December). Absence of judgement. *Policy Review*, pp. 50-54.

Pennsylvania Coalition Against Domestic Violence. (1997, September). *The impact of domestic violence*. Harrisburg: Author.

Personal Responsibility and Work Opportunity Reconciliation Act of 1996, Pub. L. 104-193, 110 Stat. 2105 (Aug. 22, 1996).

Raphael, J. (1995). *Domestic violence: Telling the untold welfare-to-work story*. Chicago: Taylor Institute.

Russell, D. (1990). *Rape in marriage* (rev. ed.). Bloomington: Indiana University Press.

Stark, E., & Flitcraft, A. (1985). Woman battering, child abuse, and social heredity: What is the relationship? In N. Johnson (Ed.), *Marital violence* (pp. 147-171). Boston: Routlege Kegan Paul.

U.S. Department of Health and Human Services [DHHS], Administration for Children and Families, Office of Public Affairs. (1997). *Change in welfare caseloads since enactment of the new welfare law*. Washington, DC: Author.

Walker, L. (1984). *The battered woman syndrome*. New York: Springer.

PART II

PARTNER ABUSE

2

The Economics of Abuse

How Violence Perpetuates Women's Poverty

Martha F. Davis

For many women, poverty is caused, exacerbated, or prolonged by abusive relationships. The following examples are typical:

> In 1992, seven months pregnant, Debby Venturella fled her abusive husband in Oklahoma and moved with her one-year-old daughter to stay with her parents and grandfather near San Francisco. She had a history of employment, but with one young child and another on the way, she was unable to get a job. When her family in California could no longer support her, she applied for public assistance, although she hadn't received welfare in Oklahoma. (*Anderson v. Green,* 1995).

> S.W. and her four children moved to Milwaukee, Wisconsin from Illinois in 1994. Over the past few years, the father of S.W.'s four children and her partner of 15 years had gotten involved with drugs and become increasingly abusive. As his violence increased, S.W. had to drop out of school and put on hold her efforts to obtain a nursing degree. On the evening of June 30, 1994, he beat S.W. with his fists and a board. S.W. and her children fled the next day. Before moving,

S.W. was working as a nursing assistant and receiving a small welfare grant from the State of Illinois. She expected that soon she would be able to stop receiving any welfare at all. Leaving home in a hurry to avoid further abuse, S.W. was able only to bring some clothing and a few personal items to Milwaukee. In dire need of housing and other basic necessities for herself and her children, S.W. turned to public assistance. (*V.C. v. Whitburn,* 1994).

After many years together, Joyce Aldridge, age 51, and her husband began experiencing marital difficulties. They obtained a legal separation. Nevertheless, Aldridge's husband continued to be verbally abusive to her. To escape continued abuse, Aldridge decided to leave North Carolina, where she and her husband had resided, and moved to New York where she could be far from her estranged husband and near her family. Aldridge stayed with her brother for several weeks, but when he sold his home, she had no place to go. Lacking housing and without funds, Aldridge applied for public assistance. (*Aumick v. Bane,* 1994).

As these case studies illustrate, adequate financial assistance—whether from family members, friends, or public assistance—often is the key factor that enables battered women and their children to leave and remain separated from their abusers. If such assistance were not available as a last resort, many battered women would be forced to remain in, or return to, dangerous or life-threatening situations.

Further, as these case studies indicate, violence affects poor women in two critical ways: it makes them poor, and it keeps them poor. In each of the cases described above, women were forced to flee from their abusers to avoid stalking and further harassment, leaving behind their homes and existing financial and emotional support networks. In addition, S.W., well on her way to moving off welfare, was forced to withdraw from nursing school because of her partner's abuse. Unfortunately, these stories are all too typical of women on welfare.

The Violence Against Women Epidemic

Violence against women has reached epidemic proportions in the United States. Between three and four million women each year are battered by husbands, partners, and boyfriends (Domestic Violence, 1994; Horn, 1992; Zorza, 1996). Half of these women are beaten severely, and in 30% of domestic violence incidents reported, assailants use weapons (Zorza, 1996). Batterers exert control over their partners' lives by force, threat of force, and emotional and economic abuse.

The epidemic is particularly acute among poor women, whose families must cope with the stress of extreme poverty, as well as other factors that contribute to violence. Although data collection is still at a relatively early stage, the cumulative evidence is becoming difficult to ignore. For example, the U.S. Department of Justice reports that, according to 1992-93 data, "women with an annual family income under $10,000 were more likely to report having experienced violence by an intimate than those with an income over $10,000" (U.S. Bureau of Justice Statistics, 1995, p. 1). Demie Kurz (1995), in her study of divorce, similarly found that poverty-level women were more likely than middle- or working-class women to have experienced frequent or serious violence within a marriage or after separation. In a Washington state survey, 60% of women on public assistance reported sexual and physical abuse as adults, usually by spouses or boyfriends (Washington State Institute for Public Policy, 1993). A Passaic County, New Jersey, study found that 57.3% of women on welfare surveyed had experienced physical abuse as adults (Raphael & Tolman, 1997). Similarly, of 436 homeless and poorly housed mothers surveyed in Massachusetts, 61% reported severe violence by male partners (Browne & Bassuk, 1997).

Most women deal with abuse by trying to leave: between 50% and 90% of battered women attempt to escape their abusive environments (Horn, 1992). Like Debby Venturella and S.W., described above, many women attempt to flee domestic violence not only to protect themselves but also to protect their children. Children of battered women are twice as likely as other children to be abused. Further, of those children who are abused, children of battered women are three times more likely to be abused by their fathers (Pagelow, 1993; *Violence Against Women,* 1990).

Women's efforts to flee, however, are often hampered and even frustrated by the economic deprivation that frequently accompanies domestic violence and by the volatile response of the abuser to the victim's departure. Abusers do not lightly relinquish control over their former partners. Typically, an abuser searches desperately for his partner once she has fled. For many abused women, the only way to stop violence that continues after separation is to move a great distance away from their abusers. Testifying before the House Subcommittee on Crime and Criminal Justice, one victim of domestic violence described her flight:

> Sixteen years ago I packed everything that would fit into a single suitcase, left behind the few possessions I owned, took my two month old baby girl and ran for my life. . . . As I got on the airplane in Dallas that day, I knew that I would never go back and that I could now begin to create a future for my daughter and myself, a future of freedom and safety. (Domestic Violence, 1994)

Unfortunately, leaving an abusive relationship does not always put an end to the violence. U.S. Department of Justice statistics show that divorced and separated women report being battered 14 times as often as women still living with their partners (Harlow, 1991). In fact, as Joyce Aldridge found when she and her husband divorced, battering and abuse often increase after separation, as batterers escalate their violence and harassment in an attempt to coerce the battered women into reconciliation or to retaliate for their departure (Mahoney, 1991; Pagelow, 1993; Wilson & Daly, 1993).

The danger of separation assault is particularly acute during the first few months of separation (Wilson & Daly, 1993). The criminal law is replete with cases describing serious bodily injury and murder committed by an abuser in response to a battered woman's flight (Pagelow, 1993). For example, in *Godfrey v. Georgia* (1980), the petitioner was convicted of murdering his wife soon after she had left the marital home and filed for divorce. The U.S. Supreme Court noted that Godfrey had abused his wife during the marriage and described the victim's departure as following a particularly violent episode.

Similarly, in a case involving the use of battered woman syndrome evidence and demonstrating the severity of separation assault against battered women, the Supreme Court of Pennsylvania detailed the history of violence between the defendant and the decedent:

> [S]he agreed to meet with him to make it clear that she did not want to see him any more. When [defendant] asked [decedent] to take her home from this meeting, [he] drove instead to a shopping center where he dragged her out of the car and then repeatedly attempted to run over her with the car. Failing to run over [her], [he] finally jumped out of the car and punched [her], breaking her nose and rendering her semi-conscious. (*Pennsylvania v. Stonehouse*, 1989)

Even escape to a shelter for victims of domestic violence is not always successful. Many batterers will stalk their victims, using personal contacts or creative resources to track down addresses of local shelters or other assistance programs (Ferraro & Johnson, 1985). In fact, many emergency assistance programs report that they have had to increase security to protect their employees from abusers who are stalking women on the premises (Raphael, 1996).

Having made the decision to flee, women in abusive relationships often must move to another community to receive crucial emotional support and transitional shelter from families and friends while they try to put their lives back in order (Bowker, 1983; Gondolf & Fisher, 1988). Many women in this position, with no place else to turn, seek help from relatives. For example, Debby Venturella left her increasingly abusive husband in Oklahoma and moved with her child to California to stay with her parents and grandfather. Once that type of help is exhausted, women such as Debby Venturella must often turn to public assistance to survive while they and their children make the transition to a new life. Indeed, data collected by the state of Wisconsin indicates that a large percentage of domestic abuse victims become welfare recipients after deciding to leave their relationships (Wisconsin Department of Administration, 1993).

Importance of Economic Support

The specific patterns and dynamics of battering contribute to women's needs for public assistance once they flee. While in abusive relationships, battered women often are subject to complete control and financial isolation by their batterers. Women frequently must leave quickly and secretly without time to pack. Women of all income levels often must leave everything behind (Davidson & Jenkins, 1989). As a result, many women must escape from their batterers with very few resources, often consisting only of money they have managed to hide or scrape together over long periods of time (Martin, 1976; Okun, 1986).

Because many domestic violence victims are economically dependent on the men who abuse them, few victims have the resources necessary to begin a new life for themselves and their children. Batterers commonly isolate battered women from financial resources (*Planned Parenthood v. Casey*, 1992). For example, many battered women do not have ready access to cash, checking accounts, or charge accounts (Lerman, 1984). One study showed that 27% of battered women had no access to cash, 34% had no access to a checking account, 51% had no access to a charge account, and 22% had no access to a car (Freedman, 1985; Horn, 1992; Walker, 1984). Women of all income levels may be affected by this economic isolation, which may itself increase the violence. According to experts on domestic violence, the more economically dependent a woman is on her batterer, the more likely she is to be at risk for serious injury (Strube & Barbour, 1983).

As an extension of this economic isolation, some batterers may forbid their partners from working outside the home (Horn, 1992; Pagelow, 1981). In one study, one third of the women surveyed reported that their batterers had prohibited them from working (Shepard & Pence, 1988). Further, although many women on welfare have ties to the workforce, violence against women is often a hidden barrier to their full job participation.

The stories of welfare-to-work program participants make clear how big a hurdle domestic violence can be for women seeking to move out of poverty. Staff at welfare-to-work programs surveyed in New York City estimated that between 30% and 75% of their clients were current or past victims of domestic violence (Kenney & Brown, 1996). Similarly, job training participants themselves report that they often cannot come to basic skills classes regularly because their attendance provokes violent behavior against them (Kenney & Brown, 1996). According to one welfare-to-work trainer interviewed in New York,

> These men are just completely threatened by the woman's involvement in the program. There is the fear that they will meet another man, a fear that this new career will take the important place in that woman's life that [the man] had held. So they are jealous and threatened by the whole experience. (Kenney & Brown, 1996, p. 16)

Post-traumatic stress disorder may also be a factor for women who have experienced abuse. Symptoms include poor concentration, diminished interest in significant activities, and a sense of foreshortened future, all of which impede efforts to move out of poverty. Similarly, the long-term physical effects of abuse can pose obstacles to women, as some are left with damaged hearing or eyesight or with chronic pain that interferes with their ability to work (Kenney & Brown, 1996).

In sum, domestic violence consumes women's time and energy and damages their self-confidence and ability to focus on long- and short-term goals, all of which are essential for a successful transition from welfare to work. As one caseworker reported, "The abuse has an impact on job readiness in part through its effect on their self-esteem—the women are not able to present themselves well in interviews and other employment situations" (Kenney & Brown, 1996, p. 18). All too often, the result is that women are overcome by these obstacles and drop out of the program (Kenney & Brown, 1996).

For those battered women who are able to work outside the home, the situation is little better. They often are forced to relinquish their earnings to batterers who insist on handling all the money in the relationships (Waits, 1985). Further, many victims must miss work because of injuries inflicted by their batterers and may lose their jobs because of the abusers' disruptive behavior (Gelles & Cornell, 1985). For example:

> One study found that 96% of women who were working while involved in an abusive relationship experienced problems at work (Zorza, 1996).
>
> One quarter of battered women surveyed had lost a job, at least partly, because of the effects of domestic violence, and over half had been harassed by their abusers at work (Zorza, 1996).
>
> A recent survey showed that 50% of abused women lost at least 3 days of work a month as a result of abuse (Freudenheim, 1988).
>
> Over 70% of employed battered women reported that their abusers harassed them at work, either in person or with repeated telephone calls (Raphael, 1996).

In the light of this information, it is not surprising that the rate of unemployment among battered women is higher than that among other women (Strube & Barbour, 1983).

Women who, despite these economic obstacles, flee abuse usually take their children with them and thus have additional financial responsibilities that contribute to poverty (Davidson & Jenkins, 1989). Because battered women may seek to protect themselves and their children by trading financial support or distribution of assets for more protective custody or limitations on the batterers' visitation with their children, they often are unable to rely on sources of support available to other single parents (Family Violence Project, 1990; Pagelow, 1993). In some instances, abused women are, justifiably, too afraid to seek child support or regular maintenance payments because they do not want any contact with their abusers (Horn, 1992). Where women do pursue child support or divorce litigation, batterers often will retaliate by waging financial warfare. A batterer may, for example, empty joint bank accounts and prolong divorce or custody proceedings to increase the victim's legal costs (Horn, 1992).

When less drastic measures have failed to stop the abuse and harassment, some women have not only fled but have "gone underground," cutting off all contact with their former lives and adopting new names. Indeed, in an effort to provide escape from the most persistent abusers, battered women's shelters and service providers have banded together, often informally, in what has been described as a modern incarnation of the "underground railroad" (Ferraro & Johnson, 1985). This enables women to flee to other cities and states and begin a violence-free life for themselves and their children. In recognition of battered women's need for secrecy as they flee under these circumstances, Congress has ordered the U.S. Postal Service to "promulgate regulations to secure the confidentiality of domestic violence shelters and abused person's addresses" (Violence Against Women Act of 1994, 1997).

Women who have been forced to take these drastic measures encounter additional, and even more acute, obstacles to financial stability. They cannot seek child support because it would alert the men stalking them to their new locations. They also cannot try to recover possessions left behind in the initial escape and may face difficulty obtaining new jobs because they cannot risk giving old employers as references for fear that either the potential employers would learn their true identities or their old employers would discover their new locations.

Clearly, battered women face significant financial obstacles as a result of their abusers' conduct toward them, particularly when children are also involved. These women and their families also must confront the economic hurdles facing all female-headed households, however, which compound the economic problems arising from abuse. By some estimates, absent parents (usually men) owe $18 billion in uncollected child support (Horn, 1992). This has a substantial negative impact on women, who head 78% of all single-parent households and 88% of poor single-parent families (Population Reference Bureau, 1993).

The wage gap and women's prevalence in low-wage occupations exacerbates these problems. In 1989 in the United States, the median family income for single-mother-headed households was $12,000, whereas that for married couples with children was $41,000 (U.S. Department of Commerce, 1990). In the third quarter of 1994, women who worked full time earned only 77.9% of the median earnings for men (U.S. Bureau of Labor Statistics, 1994). Working poor women face the additional cost of child care, which often amounts to 25% of their income; for nonpoor families, child care costs represent less than 6% of their income (House Committee on Ways and Means, 1996).

In sum, women's escape from violence in their own homes is dependent, to a great extent, on available financial resources. Without adequate income support, women who leave battering relationships face a high risk of becoming homeless. Services targeted to battered women often provide only emergency or transitional help lasting a few weeks, insufficient to allow women to support their families and move toward economic independence (House Committee on Ways and Means, 1996). Indeed, battered women with or without children make up a significant portion of the homeless population (Mascari, 1987; Zorza, 1991). According to one recent study of low-income women in Massachusetts, 92% of those who were homeless had experienced severe physical violence or sexual assault some time in their lives (Bassuk, Browne, & Buckner, 1996).

Many women remain trapped in abusive relationships because they lack the resources to leave and fear the poverty they may face. Without access to the support necessary to survive at a minimal level and faced with poverty and homelessness, battered women, particularly those with children, must

> balance the possible harm to the children through inadequate housing with the harm from maintaining the bettering relationships. Unless the children are threatened directly or indirectly, a woman may well choose for them, rather than for herself. In a very real way, she is choosing between known and unknown dangers. (Mahoney, 1991)

Further, battered women who leave even severely violent relationships often return to their batterers for economic reasons (*Planned Parenthood v. Casey,* 1992). Indeed, the Wisconsin Department of Administration (1993) reports that lack of affordable housing in many Wisconsin communities has forced domestic abuse victims without other options to return to their abusive situations. Without adequate financial assistance, battered women are too often forced to accept violence as an inevitable fact of life. Clearly, to afford to live safely and separately from their abusive partners, battered women must have a "sound bridge out of poverty" (Gondolf & Fisher, 1988).

Policy Responses

The realities of violence in women's lives suggest the need for federal, state, and local welfare programs that are quite different from those recently enacted by Congress in the federal welfare reform bill of 1996. First, welfare-to-work programs should be designed to provide flexibility and support for poor women experiencing violence. Some programs have already taken steps in this direction. For example, the Family Support and Education Center in Cecil County, Maryland, persuaded the local domestic violence center to provide services directly at the welfare center job-training site (Raphael, 1995). Similarly, the Young Adult Learning Academy in New York is making efforts to lengthen program cycles so that staff can have more time to work intensively with participants and therefore increase the chances of helping a participant leave an abusive relationship. Another New York program, the Mid-Bronx Head Start program, is making strategic efforts to work with fathers as well as mothers of Head Start children. Caseworkers believe that, by offering counseling, job training, and job placements to the men, Head Start can eliminate some ways the program is viewed as alien and threatening and, therefore, as a stimulus for abuse (Kenney & Brown, 1996).

In addition, many states have signaled their initial willingness to address these issues by adopting the Family Violence Option of the federal Personal Responsibility and Work Opportunity Reconciliation Act (see Chapter 1). When taken, that state option provides states with flexibility in applying time limits, work requirements, and other federal and state mandates to domestic violence survivors (NOW Legal Defense and Education Fund, 1997). Advocates are working with state and local welfare agencies to ensure that this flexibility is implemented in ways that will help battered women. In short, government can clearly play a constructive role by designing and funding programs that recognize this crucial need and by ensuring that new welfare reform programs enhance, rather than undercut, these efforts.

Second, to implement these programs responsibly, state and federal governments must have accurate information and develop procedures that permit battered women to come forward safely. One key problem currently facing battered women on welfare is the risk of sanctions or reduced welfare benefits if the agency becomes aware that they have live-in partners or boyfriends. For example, the partner's income may, under certain circumstances, be attributed to the woman and her children even if the partner does not contribute to the household finances. Although reporting rules are intended to target subsidies to those who are most in need, state-level reform is clearly necessary to ensure that these rules do not serve as a deterrent to reporting violence while at the same time frustrating efforts to identify the real barriers that keep women poor.

Third, because policymakers have generally ignored the role that violence plays in the lives of poor women, some new welfare reform provisions may have the effect of exacerbating women's poverty. For instance, two-tiered benefit schemes, in which women who move between states are generally paid lower benefits (at the level set by their prior state), may deter women from fleeing battering and from leaving abusive situations to join family and friends far outside the reach of their abusers (Davis & Kraham, 1995). Similarly, mandates that teenage parents live at home in order to receive Temporary Assistance to Needy Families (TANF) and states' narrowing of the "good cause" exceptions to women's obligation to participate in identifying paternity limit women's ability to make decisions about housing and paternity establishment that reflect their own knowledge of their situation and assessment of the risk of violence. Increasing the potential for violence by ignoring the violent realities of women's lives will only increase the risk to women and their families while prolonging their need for public assistance.

Finally, adequate public assistance support is clearly a necessary part of efforts to eliminate violence against women. Welfare benefits are already far from adequate. Yet, without the minimal safety net provided by public assistance, women and children simply cannot leave violent situations. According to the federal government's own measures, the average monthly benefit measured in 1995 dollars fell from $713 in 1970 to $377 in 1995, a 47% drop (House Committee on Ways and Means, 1996). The future of benefit levels is largely in the hands of the states.

A federally mandated lifetime limit of welfare benefits to 5 years (or less) makes no sense in the light of this function of welfare—that is, to provide the economic safety net that battered women need in order to escape abuse. Women may experience violence throughout their lifetimes and, depending on the individual circumstances, may need to rely on government assistance longer than any arbitrary time limit. As time limits are nevertheless imposed by states, women faced with choosing between beatings and starvation may too often choose beatings, exposing themselves and their children to prolonged abuse that will perpetuate both violence and poverty.

References

Anderson v. Green, 811 F. Supp. 516 (E.D. Cal. 1993) (No. Civ-S-92-2118), aff'd, 26 F.3d 95 (9th Cir. 1994), vacated, 513 U.S. 557 (1995). Affidavit of Debby Venturella.

Aumick v. Bane, 161 Misc. 2d 271 (N.Y. Sup. Ct., Monroe Co., 1994), Proposed Intervenor Petition.

Bassuk, E. L., Browne, A., & Buckner, J. C. (1996, October). Single mothers and welfare. *Scientific American, 275*(4), 60-67.

Bowker, L. H. (1983). *Beating wife beating.* Lexington, MA: Lexington.

Browne, A., & Bassuk, S. (1997). Intimate violence in the lives of homeless and poorly housed women: Prevalence and patterns in an ethnically diverse sample. *American Journal of Orthopsychiatry, 6*(2), 261-278.

Davidson, B., & Jenkins, P. (1989). Class diversity in shelter life. *Social Work, 3*(4), 491-495.

Davis, M. F., & Kraham, S. J. (1995, January 13). Beaten, then robbed. *New York Times,* p. A31.

Domestic violence: Not just a family matter: Hearing before the Subcommittee on Crime and Criminal Justice of the House Committee on the Judiciary, 103rd Cong., 2nd Sess. (1994, June 30).

Family Violence Project. (1990). *Family violence: Improving court practices* (Recommendations from the National Council of Juvenile and Family Court Judges' Family Violence Project).

Ferraro, K., & Johnson, J. (1985). The new underground railroad. *Studies in Symbolic Interaction, 6,* 377-386.

Freedman, L. (1985). Wife assault. In C. Guberman & M. Wolfe (Eds.), *No safe place* (pp. 41-60). Toronto: Women's Press.

Freudenheim, M. (1988, August 23). Employers act to stop family violence. *New York Times,* p. A1.

Gelles, R., & Cornell, C. P. (1985). *Intimate violence in families.* Beverly Hills, CA: Sage.

Godfrey v. Georgia, 446 U.S. 420 (1980).

Gondolf, E. W., & Fisher, E. R. (1988). *Battered women as survivors: An alternative to treating learned helplessness.* Lexington, MA: Lexington.

Harlow, C. (1991). *Female victims of violent crime.* Washington, DC: U.S. Department of Justice.

Horn, P. (1992, December). Beating back the revolution. *Dollars and Sense,* p. 12.

House Committee on Ways and Means, 104th Cong., 2d Sess., (1996). *1996 green book.* Washington, DC: Government Printing Office.

Kenney, C. T., & Brown, K. R. (1996). *Report from the front lines: The impact of violence on poor women.* New York: NOW Legal Defense and Education Fund.

Kurz, D. (1995). *For richer, for poorer: Mothers confront divorce.* New York: Routledge.

Lerman, L. G. (1984). A model state act: Remedies for domestic abuse. *Harvard Journal on Legislation, 21,* 61.

Mahoney, M. R. (1991). Legal images of battered women: Redefining the issue of separation. *Michigan Law Review, 90,* 1.

Martin, D. (1976). *Battered wives.* San Francisco: Glide.

Mascari, D. (1987). Comment, homeless families: Do they have a right to integrity? *UCLA Law Review, 35,* 159-204.

NOW Legal Defense and Education Fund. (1997). *The Family Violence Option in the new welfare law.* New York: Author.

Okun, L. (1986). *Woman abuse: Facts replacing myths.* Albany: State University of New York Press.

Pagelow, M. (1993). Justice for victims of spouse abuse in divorce and child custody cases. *Violence and Victims, 8*(1), 69-83.

Pagelow, M. D. (1981). *Women battering: Victims and their experiences.* Beverly Hills, CA: Sage.

Pennsylvania v. Stonehouse, 521 Pa. 41, 555 A.2d 772 (1989).

Planned Parenthood v. Casey, 505 U.S. 833 (1992).

Population Reference Bureau, Inc. (1993). *What the 1990 census tells us about women: A state factbook.* Washington, DC: Author.

Raphael, J. (1995, January). *Domestic violence: Telling the untold welfare-to-work story.* Chicago: Taylor Institute.

Raphael, J. (1996, April). *Prisoners of abuse: Domestic violence and welfare receipt.* Chicago: Taylor Institute.

Raphael, J., & Tolman, R. (1997). *Trapped by poverty, trapped by abuse: New evidence documenting the relationship between domestic violence and welfare.* Chicago: Taylor Institute.

Shepard, M., & Pence, E. (1988). The effect of battering on the employment status of women. *Affilia, 3,* 55-61.

Strube, M. J., & Barbour, L. S. (1983). The decision to leave an abusive relationship: Economic dependence and psychological commitment. *Journal of Marriage and the Family, 45*(4), 785-793.

U.S. Bureau of Justice Statistics. (1995). *Violence against women: Estimates from the redesigned survey.* Washington, DC: Author.

U.S. Bureau of Labor Statistics. (1994, October 26) *Usual weekly earnings of wage and salary workers: Third quarter 1994.* Washington, DC: Author.

U.S. Department of Commerce, Bureau of the Census. (1990). *Social and economic characteristics.* Washington, DC: Author.

V.C. v. Whitburn, No. 94-C-1028 (E.D. Wis., filed September 13, 1994), Affidavit of Plaintiff S.W.

Violence against women: Domestic violence hearing before the Senate Judiciary Committee, 101st Cong., 2nd Sess. 7 (1990, December 11).

Violence Against Women Act of 1994, 42 U.S.C. Sec. 13951 (1997).

Waits, K. (1985). The criminal justice system's response to battering: Understanding the problem, forging the solutions. *Washington Law Review, 60,* 267-329.

Walker, L. (1984). *The battered woman syndrome.* New York: Springer.

Washington State Institute for Public Policy. (1993). *Over half of women on public assistance in Washington State reported physical or sexual abuse as adults.* Olympia: Author.

Wilson, M., & Daly, M. (1993). Spousal homicide risk and estrangement. *Violence and Victims, 8,* 3.

Wisconsin Department of Administration, Division of Housing. (1993, November 1). *State of Wisconsin 1994-1998 comprehensive housing affordability strategy.*

Zorza, J. (1991). Woman battering: A major cause of homelessness. *Clearinghouse Review, 25,* 421-429.

Zorza, J. (1996). Women battering: High costs and the state of the law. *Clearinghouse Review, 28,* 383-395.

3

Keeping Women Poor

How Domestic Violence Prevents Women From Leaving Welfare and Entering the World of Work

Jody Raphael

Evelyn, a former heroin addict, needs methadone in order to function. Because she is on a waiting list for a free methadone maintenance clinic, her intimate partner pays for the drug. Evelyn enrolled in a literacy program, but as she got closer to getting her GED (high school equivalency), her partner began to feel threatened by her progress and her plans to get a job. When she refused to quit the program at his insistence, he simply stopped buying her methadone. Evelyn was forced to drop out of the literacy program in order to maintain her physical well-being.

Sabotage? Yes. Domestic violence? Yes. Within the past few years, program providers working with low-income girls and women have come to realize that domestic violence is a major welfare-to-work barrier. Threatened by the independence of their partners, some men

31

use threats of violence, violence itself, and sabotage like that in Evelyn's case to keep their partners from education, training, and employment. Providers have also noted that the effects of past violence serve as major barriers to work, including depression and anxiety, as well as the more full-blown symptoms of post-traumatic stress disorder (PTSD).

Some current and past victims of domestic violence receiving welfare will have difficulty when the violence prevents them from complying with their states' new work requirements within the context of new transitional welfare systems. It appears likely that because some victims will not be able to enter the labor market, they will lose their welfare benefits and, as a result, will remain locked in the arms of their abusers. Still others may try to work or participate in job-training programs but will return home to be faced with violence and sabotage. In this era of welfare reform, therefore, it is important for all practitioners working with low-income women and their children to understand better the role that domestic violence plays in making and keeping women and children poor.

This chapter explores the patterns of violence and abuse that sabotage women's welfare-to-work journeys. I summarize my own research, consisting of interviews in programs throughout the country (Raphael, 1995, 1996; Raphael & Tolman, 1997) and corroborated by a research study in New York City (Kenney & Brown, 1996), all of which reveal consistent patterns of violence and sabotage during the welfare-to-work transition. Next, I explain what new research can tell us about the extent of the problem within state welfare caseloads. Last, I outline the policy and service responses that are necessary for meeting the needs of domestic violence victims on welfare.

Patterns of Sabotage and Abuse

In-Home Sabotage

Interviews with welfare-to-work program participants and staff reveal consistent and multiple instances of male sabotage of women's welfare-to-work efforts. Although the variety of methods and devices used by these men to keep women at home and out of the workplace

are startling, even more astonishing is the consistency of these practices throughout the country:

> Women's partners surreptitiously turn off the alarm clocks set by the
> women to make sure they would be on time for job interviews
> (Raphael, 1996).
>
> Partners cut off the women's hair because they believe, correctly, that the
> women would be too embarrassed to return to work (Raphael, 1996).
>
> Partners inflict visible injuries such as black eyes and cigarette burns,
> hoping the women will not return to the training program out of
> embarrassment and will be expelled for nonattendance or unex-
> plained absences. "My father would inflict black eyes, bruises all over
> my mother's body, and knock her teeth out. My mom couldn't go to
> work and was ashamed to be around any of her friends because of
> the way she looked," explains one welfare participant (Raphael,
> 1996, p. 6).
>
> Women's partners hide or destroy books or tear up completed homework
> assignments (Raphael, 1996).
>
> Men hide or destroy their partners' clothing, including winter coats, so
> that they are unable to leave the home to take a GED test or to
> complete an important job interview. "My abuser stole all my
> clothes," explains one woman. "All my work uniforms. I worked in
> hotels and they all had the same blue uniforms. So all my uniforms,
> all my dress clothes. I couldn't even go to a job interview because all
> I had was a pair of jeans. I couldn't go anywhere decent until I finally
> got help" (Raphael & Tolman, 1997, p. 12).
>
> Men sabotage their partners' forms of transportation. "They don't want
> you to better yourself. It was my first semester at college and he
> started working on my car and making it to where my car wouldn't
> run so I couldn't get to school, because he knew that if I got to school,
> that I would better myself and that I wouldn't need him. You know,
> that I could survive without him and support myself. And that was a
> threat to him," explained another (Raphael & Tolman, 1997, p. 12).
>
> Partners promise to provide needed child care so that the women can
> attend a special career event, such as a job fair or an interview, but
> fail to show up or arrive inebriated when needed (Raphael, 1996).
>
> Partners harass the women at their place of employment so that they are
> fired or are forced to quit. The men come around uninvited, refuse
> to leave, or harass the women with numerous telephone calls. "He
> called them and told them that I was to quit and I was to quit right
> then. And he made a horrible scene. My employer can't have things
> like that going on, you know," explained one welfare participant
> (Raphael & Tolman, 1997, p. 10). Another woman was forced by her
> abuser to quit the job she had obtained at a local school. "He kept
> accusing me of having an affair with the school bus driver," she stated,

and because of the physical and mental abuse, she quit the job (personal interview, January 27, 1997).

The most common form of male sabotage uncovered in the Taylor Institute's research is the practice of getting into fights and inflicting violence the night or morning before key events such as a GED test or a job interview. One woman's partner instigated a major argument and inflicted severe physical abuse the night before the final examination in her licensed practical nursing course. Sleep-deprived and pro-foundly depressed by the renewed onset of the abuse, she failed the test and was unable to continue in the program (Raphael, 1996).

A case manager at a literacy program gives two examples of this kind of sabotage:

> The abuser argues with my client before school every day. She can't concentrate. I have to talk to her every morning to calm her down and focus her. I have another client who is close to getting her GED. He broke her right arm (she's right-handed). As soon as it healed he broke it again and she was in a cast again. You have to call it sabotage—its not just anger. Women have to recognize it for what it is. (Raphael & Tolman, 1997, p. 12)

Writes Karen Brown, formerly with the City Works Program at Bronx Community College (Bronx, New York):

> Often students will get into altercations with their partners before such crucial events, causing them either to miss the event altogether or arrive in such an agitated state that their performance is compro-mised. After this became a pattern I personally began to suspect that it was not a coincidence that these events were occurring right before the important job-related event that was important for the student. (Raphael, 1996, p. 6)

Another job placement counselor reports:

> We sent one participant out for a job interview, but she did not show up. When we called to follow up with her, she told us that her partner had proceeded to drive her to the interview. He was not quite happy that she was going to be working or even trying to get out and find employment for herself. They started arguing and one thing led to another and he started hitting her. So by the time she did get out there she was beaten up. He drove her half-way back and let her out, and she had to hitchhike the rest of the way home. She has now obtained

a job but comes home and gets beaten. She feels that she cannot abandon him. He is a recovering addict who tells her that she is the only person that he has. She is a victim of both physical abuse and emotional blackmail. (Raphael & Tolman, 1997, p. 12)

Threats of death and suicide are the ultimate weapon of sabotage. The Worcester Family Research Project, for example, found that, in 26.4% of its homeless AFDC sample and 18.1% of its housed AFDC sample, the male partner threatened to kill himself (Raphael & Tolman, 1997). The following true story is, unfortunately, typical of what can happen when a battered women decides to leave an abusive relationship. The welfare department worker explains:

After five years together, my client told her abuser she was leaving. In the presence of the woman and her two children, ages three and two, he threatened to kill her and her unborn child by sticking a gun into her womb. Then, turning the gun on himself, he took his own life in front of them. My client had a miscarriage and is now in therapy. She is extremely angry for allowing herself to be in the situation and feeling guilty and responsible for what happened at the same time. (Raphael & Tolman, 1997, p. 12)

Leaving the Violence: Harassment and Stalking

Unfortunately, leaving a violent relationship is often not the end of the violence, but rather marks the beginning of an escalation of domestic violence. Crime statistics bear out the fact that it is more dangerous for the woman and her family after she has left the abuser than before. Although divorced and separated women make up only 10% of all women in the United States, they account for 75% of all battered women and report being battered 14 times as often as women still living with their partners (U.S. Department of Justice, 1991).

One literacy program participant described the time when her ex-partner met her coming out of her literacy program, grabbed her by the hair, threw her into the car, and kidnapped her by force for a 48-hour period. "I am determined to get my GED. The only way I won't get it is if he kidnaps me and takes me. He's done it before" (Raphael, 1996, p. 8).

Stalking seriously interferes with the participants' ability to perform at job training or on the job. Explained one victim, who had left her abuser and moved in with a supportive uncle, "I was constantly aggravated. I couldn't function. I couldn't sit, I couldn't think, I was always wondering, if I walk out of this building, is he going to be outside? I finally had enough courage to lock him up" (Raphael, 1996, p. 9).

A former welfare participant reported that she had been applying for jobs, unsuccessfully, over a 2-year period. Eventually, she noticed that she was being trailed by a particular van. When the license plate was checked, she discovered that it was a surveillance company hired by her former boyfriend. She discovered that he would then call the potential employer and say whatever it would take to make certain she would not be hired. Only when she was able to halt this behavior was she able to land a job (Raphael, 1996, p. 9).

Participants report that their former partners trump up police charges or child abuse charges against them, requiring them to attend numerous court appearances, resulting in job losses (Raphael, 1996). Enrolled in a training program after she separated from her abuser, one welfare participant explained that he called the Department of Family Services to complain that she was abusing her daughter:

> I made an appointment to meet the worker so he could come investigate us for 8:00 Monday morning because I had to get to school. And that Sunday night he came and we had a horrible assault situation. I'm pressing charges at 4:00 in the morning at the police station, and before that I had to take my daughter to my mother's house because I don't want her to go to the police station. I didn't even have time to go to the emergency room until the next afternoon because I had to meet the worker at 8:00 in the morning and then go to school. This abuse causes me to miss school all the time and I couldn't tell all these people, so I had to come up with reasons as to why. And now I think, I can't believe that I was assaulted and was actually grateful that it was just my body and not my face, I didn't have any bruises. With the police station, the 8:00 thing and then school, I couldn't even go to the emergency room. (Raphael & Tolman, 1997, p. 10)

Harassment at the job site is a particularly common form of abuse. Because the women have left their relationships, a worksite may be the only place where such abuse can take place. If women keep their jobs, they risk being shadowed by their abusers as they leave work, which results in their new whereabouts being discovered and in further violence.

Some survivors of domestic violence report that their abusers try to get back at them by threatening to kidnap their children. Leaving children in child care centers can be problematic for these survivors. "I was always scared that he would go get my children from their day care and schools and things like that, so there was that kind of stress too," explains one former battered woman (Raphael & Tolman, 1997, p. 8).

Karen's case epitomizes how domestic violence continues to plague past victims and to interfere with their employment. Karen had evicted her abusive partner, who was seriously addicted to drugs, and obtained a part-time job supplemented by a small welfare grant. Her order of protection was not enough to prevent him from coming by her apartment in a public housing project one evening, after which he beat her up, broke her arm, and took the money she had laid aside for the rent at the first of the month. Because no shelter space was available in Chicago, the next day she was taken to a hotel room in the western suburbs in a program operated by a suburban domestic violence program. The hotel now housing Karen and her children is so far away that Karen is not able to get to work. Her coworkers are desperately trying to find a shelter bed for Karen that is on a bus line to her job. Karen's abuser has threatened to kill her, so a return to her apartment is not feasible.

The Ongoing Effects of Domestic Violence

Welfare-to-work programs report that the physical and mental effects of past violence serve as major barriers to labor market participation. Some victims suffer from depression or persistent anxiety that seriously affects their ability to seek and hold employment. Others may suffer from the more serious symptoms of PTSD, which involves reliving or reexperiencing the trauma, the numbing of responses, or increased arousal, demonstrated by an inability to sleep, focus, or concentrate (Herman, 1992).

A letter I recently received from a domestic violence survivor provides a complete picture of how past violence can continue to play a current role:

> I was a tenured professor on a research grant in Italy when I met my ex-husband. Within a few months, my productivity suffered significantly due to emotional turmoil, lack of sleep, and the demands he

made upon the flexibility of my writing schedule. . . . When I returned to full-time teaching and took on the responsibility of department chair . . . he made things difficult for me professionally by such antics as abusing me all night before important meetings, making me late for meetings, and intimidating me about conversing with male colleagues in my department. . . . Once he made me miss a meeting by closing the garage door before I was able to pull the car out and then threatening me with a can of gasoline until I turned the car off and talked to him for another hour. . . . I returned to work the next academic year, overriding my inner wisdom, due to fear of having no income and started to deteriorate physically and psychologically. By December I was having suicidal ideation; by March, I was in bed every waking hour . . . due to environmental and food allergies, psychotropic drug reactions, and the exhaustion of being in a constant state of hyperarousal. By May I was able to support my claim for disability on the SSI program. (Raphael & Tolman, 1997, p. 4)

Memories of domestic violence can also continue to reoccur, often with paralyzing results. Explained one domestic violence survivor:

The last Valentine's Day we were together my husband had raped me. This Valentine's Day the memory came up and hit me over the head. I was almost catatonic—it was just left-over trauma. It's really difficult to put your life together again because there's so much pressure just to survive, to provide food and clothing for your child. If you try to do that and don't deal with the psychological issues at the same time, it's self-defeating. Someday that stuff will catch up with you. . . . Leaving—it's not just walking out one day and okay, that's the end of it. . . . I've been out of the relationship three years, and I'm just starting to deal with the trauma. It's difficult for me to trust anybody. I assume if anybody promises to do something, they'll probably back out of it. Even normal day-to-day interaction with people is exhausting. There's no way you can rebuild your life in two years. (Raphael & Tolman, 1997, p. 4)

Thoughts of suicide can be a common response to domestic violence. According to one job counselor, when one of her program participants, a survivor of domestic violence, was confronted with the pressure of going on job interviews as part of a welfare-department-mandated job search, she locked herself in the program's bathroom and attempted to slit her wrists. Later, with the assistance of inpatient and outpatient therapy and medication, she was able to hold down two part-time cashier jobs and leave welfare (Raphael & Tolman, 1997).

Another welfare-to-work participant, a survivor of domestic violence enrolled in a junior college paralegal training program, now takes three psychotropic medications. The bruising and jarring of her brain, along with eye injuries, cause frequent and intolerable headaches. She needs to develop the organizational skills necessary for successful school completion. Because of her abuse, she was never able to plan her life:

> Any minute or hour of any given day, I could be dead. I saw no importance to it. My life was fear, insecurity, confusion, uncertainty, worry, pain, and many days of wishing I was dead, since death was the final escape. . . . I still encounter physical and mental barriers and I always will. (Raphael, 1996, p. 3)

Other survivors report problems completing tasks at work because of the traumatic effects of domestic violence. Explains one,

> I have trouble at work as a result of past domestic violence. I have a communications defect. I don't feel I am educated enough to get my points across. I am always writing my points down. I worry that I am always missing something. I am always watching for an attack so I am on guard all the time and I am not really listening. I am always needing to ask for clarification and that angers people on the job. (Raphael & Tolman, 1997, p. 10)

Explains another,

> They tell me I wouldn't make decisions on the job without somebody okaying. I could not make decision on my own. That's the biggest drawback that I've had, learning how to make decisions and feeling comfortable with what I can do. (Raphael & Tolman, 1997, p. 8)

Determining the Extent of the Problem

Until recently, researchers have depended on data from welfare-to-work programs to estimate the extent of the problem of domestic violence within welfare caseloads. Now, results from four recent in-depth studies, each involving fairly large samples, provide a more accurate answer to the question of the extent of current and past domestic violence among women receiving welfare. All of these studies were published in reports in 1996 and 1997:

1. *The Passaic County Study of AFDC Recipients in a Welfare-to-Work Program,* a sample of 846 women on AFDC in a mandatory pre-employment training program between December 1995 and January 1997 (Curcio, 1997).

   14.6% of the sample reported current physical abuse by an intimate partner and 25% verbal or emotional abuse, with 57.3% of the entire sample reporting physical abuse sometime during their adulthood.

   12.9% of the entire sample, and 39.7% of those current abuse victims, reported that their partners actively prevent their participation in education and training.

2. *In Harm's Way? Domestic Violence, AFDC Receipt, and Welfare Reform in Massachusetts,* a random sample of 734 women in the current state caseload, surveyed between January and June 1996 by the University of Massachusetts, Boston. This study is the first scientific sampling of one state's entire AFDC caseload that measured both current and past prevalence of domestic violence (Allard, Colten, Albelda, & Cosenza, 1997).

   19.5% of the sample reported current physical violence at the hands of an intimate partner, with 64% experiencing intimate partner violence ever in life as an adult.

   This study supports the contention that perpetrators of violence interfere with women's attempts to comply with welfare work requirements. Abused women in the sample were 10 times more likely than their never-abused counterparts to have current partners who would not like them going to school or work (15.5% vs. 1.6%).

3. *The Worcester Family Research Project,* a 5-year study of 436 homeless and housed women, most of whom received AFDC, in Worcester, Massachusetts, conducted by the Better Homes Fund between August 1992 and July 1995 (Bassuk et al., 1996).

   The study found that, of the entire sample of homeless and housed women, 61% had been severely physically assaulted by intimate male partners as adults and that nearly one third (32%) had experienced severe violence from their current or most recent partners. Over one third (34%) had been threatened with death by their intimate partners.

   This research also showed current high prevalences of mental health problems and PTSD within the entire welfare sample at levels two to three times that in the general female population. Because of the high percentages of battered women in the sample, it is likely that some victims were suffering from these effects of trauma.

4. *The Effects of Violence on Women's Employment,* a random survey of 824 women in one low-income neighborhood of Chicago, conducted by the Joint Center for Poverty Research at Northwestern University between September 1994 and May 1995 (Lloyd, 1996).

   Although rates of domestic violence were high for the entire neighborhood sample (11.8%), AFDC recipients experienced 3 times the amount of physical violence that their non-AFDC neighborhood counterparts within the last year (31.3%) and 2.4 times the amount of severe physical aggression within the last year (19.5% vs. 8.1%).

These four studies clearly demonstrate that domestic violence is a factor in a high percentage of welfare recipients' lives. Current domestic violence victims represent 14.6% to 32% of these welfare samples, and approximately 60% of the samples are composed of past victims of domestic violence (Raphael & Tolman, 1997). The patterns of sabotage described by the qualitative research are corroborated by this new research. High percentages of abused women in the Massachusetts caseload survey reported arguments about child support (30%), visitation (23%), and child custody (14.7%), and police visits to their homes (36%), as well as interference from their intimate partners with education, training, and work (Allard et al., 1997). In the Passaic County study, three times as many currently abused women as nonabused women stated that their intimate partners actively tried to prevent them from obtaining education or training (39.7% vs. 12.9% for the entire sample) (Curcio, 1997).

Policy and Service Delivery Implications

This new research does not provide definitive answers necessary to frame effective policy and service delivery responses. For this, we need to know more about the abusive men in these women's lives. It is important to understand better why some men are so threatened by the employment of their partners. In the context of current welfare policies, some men who are themselves uneducated, unemployed, or underemployed may feel abandoned by governmental programs; this feeling may increase their need to control and dominate their partners. It is not known whether, in addition to criminal justice sanctions, interventions geared to helping men develop themselves in the labor market could be useful in eliminating domestic violence.

Nor does the research assist us in determining what strategies will be able to help battered women on welfare become economically self-sufficient. As is apparent from the wide variety of methods by which abusive men sabotage their partners' efforts to become economically independent, it is essential that service providers and policymakers not overgeneralize about battered women. For many battered women, work is the only way they can permanently escape violence.

Rather than an exemption from work, they need better supports and assistance to enter the workforce and to maintain employment. Some battered women will be able to comply with welfare requirements if well-structured welfare-to-work programs are available to them. Many dealing with abusive partners may be successful only if they have increased safety planning and domestic violence services. Others, because of the severity of the threat, the likelihood of escalation of violence, or the traumatic effects of the violence, will need short-term or long-term waivers of welfare work requirements.

As a result, welfare policy at the state level must be flexible enough to ensure that each battered woman receives the services she needs in order to take the appropriate pathway toward work that does not further endanger herself or her children. This policy result is in no way precluded by the new federal welfare legislation.

Each community, however, must develop a network of needed services for battered women and their children. Without these services, all the good assessment and sensitive welfare policy in the world will not meet the needs of battered women on welfare. Battered women need a variety of services, including counseling and safety planning; legal services; emergency housing; vocational counseling; literacy and job training; mental health services; and alcohol and drug treatment. Specialized support for battered women can also be structured effectively within the context of welfare-to-work and job-training programs. In serving battered women within the welfare system, it is important that these efforts be coordinated with agencies serving abused women in the community. Partnerships with battered women's advocates who have experience and expertise in serving domestic violence victims are crucial.

Given the prevalence of domestic violence within welfare caseloads, it is incumbent upon every helping professional and every welfare department worker to become trained in domestic violence. Because of the pervasiveness of the problem among low-income girls and women, all agencies serving low-income populations must be specially trained in domestic violence and its assessment.

It is now time for service providers and policymakers to become more aware of the role that domestic violence plays in keeping low-income girls and women trapped in poverty. Because domestic violence is a hidden secret, one rarely shared with others, those in the helping professions cannot assume that domestic violence is not present if it is not mentioned by their clients. It is time to connect what we know about domestic violence with antipoverty efforts. Not only does the failure to take domestic violence into account cause conventional antipoverty interventions to fail, but it also can make life even more difficult and dangerous for girls and women. We must all learn to feel more comfortable with talking about domestic violence and helping girls and women eliminate it from their lives.

References

Allard, M. A., Colten, M. E., Albelda, R., & Cosenza, C. (1997). *In harm's way? Domestic violence, AFDC receipt, and welfare reform in Massachusetts.* Boston: University of Massachusetts, McCormack Institute, Center for Survey Research.

Bassuk, E., Weinreb, L., Buckner, J., Browne, A., Salomon, A., & Bassuk, S. (1996). The characteristics and needs of sheltered homeless and low-income housed mothers. *Journal of the American Medical Association, 276*(8), 640-646.

Curcio, W. (1997). *The Passaic County study of AFDC recipients in a welfare-to-work program: A preliminary analysis.* Paterson, NJ: Passaic County Board of Social Services.

Herman, J. (1992). *Trauma and recovery.* New York: Basic Books.

Kenney, C., & Brown, K. (1996). *Report from the front lines: The impact of violence on poor women.* New York: NOW Legal Defense and Education Fund.

Lloyd, S. (1996). *The effects of violence on women's employment.* Evanston, IL: Northwestern University, Joint Center for Poverty Research and Institute for Policy Research.

Raphael, J. (1995). *Domestic violence: Telling the untold welfare-to-work story.* Chicago: Taylor Institute.

Raphael, J. (1996). *Prisoners of abuse: Domestic violence and welfare receipt.* Chicago: Taylor Institute.

Raphael J., & Tolman, R. (1997). *Trapped by poverty/Trapped by abuse: New evidence documenting the relationship between domestic violence and welfare.* Chicago: Taylor Institute and the University of Michigan Research Development Center on Poverty, Risk, and Mental Health.

U.S. Department of Justice. (1991). *Female victims of violent crimes 5.* Washington, DC: Government Printing Office.

4

Family Violence and Welfare Use

Report From the Field

Ruth A. Brandwein

On August 22, 1996, President Bill Clinton signed a historic piece of legislation. The Personal Responsibility and Work Opportunity Reconciliation of 1996 (PRA) ended 60 years of federal government entitlements to poor mothers and their children. It represents the most fundamental change in the safety net since the creation of Aid to Dependent Children (ADC) as part of the 1935 Social Security Act. It is described briefly in the first chapter of this book, and its implications are fully examined in the concluding chapter.

During the years of discussion and debate preceding enactment of this legislation, rhetoric about the clients of the welfare system had escalated. They had been stereotyped as lazy freeloaders bearing

AUTHOR'S NOTE: I thank Anissa Rogers and Diana Filiano for their invaluable assistance in entering and analyzing data and helping with the focus groups. I am also grateful for the unstinting support and cooperation of the Salt lake City Police Department, the Utah Department of Human Services, the Salt Lake City YWCA, and JEDI Women.

numerous children to collect welfare. Welfare itself was castigated as causing dependency (Gilder, 1981; Kaus, 1992; Murray, 1984). Legislators argued that setting timetables and then cutting mothers off from welfare would help them assume responsibility for their own families. Even David Ellwood (1988), a professor at the Kennedy School in Cambridge, Massachusetts, who became President Clinton's first assistant secretary for planning and evaluation at the Department of Health and Human Services, called for a 2-year limit on welfare prior to requiring recipients to work.

If women targeted by "welfare reform" are victims of domestic violence, how the public views them and the policies for providing them with assistance would need to be dramatically changed. If welfare is a path out of an abusive relationship, what will be the effects of more stringent requirements recently enacted in the new welfare reform law? This legislation includes policies such as lifetime limits on the use of welfare, mandatory work requirements, residency requirements that would punish women moving to another state, family caps that provide no additional support for any children born after a woman is on welfare, and loss of financial support for failing to provide information about a child's father to the child support enforcement worker.

Review of the Literature

In the last few years, researchers have been gathering data that support the premise that welfare clients and domestic violence victims are often one and the same. Researchers at the McCormack Institute at the University of Massachusetts interviewed a representative sample of Massachusetts women receiving Aid to Families With Dependent Children (AFDC) between January and June of 1996. They found that 20% of women interviewed had experienced abuse by intimate partners or former partners within the past 12 months and that 65% had been such victims in their lifetimes (Allard, Colten, Albelda, & Cosenza, 1997).

A representative sample of Washington AFDC recipients interviewed in 1992 reported that 55% had been physically or sexually abused by spouses or boyfriends, compared with 28% of a random sample of a comparison group (Washington State Institute for Public Policy, 1993).

In a Utah study of AFDC recipients, 57% reported having been sexually abused, either as children or as adults. In response to a question about current barriers to self-sufficiency, 17% identified abusive partners, 38% identified emotional or physical disabilities, and 34% identified children's behavioral problems, which are often the result of domestic violence (University of Utah Survey Research Center, 1993).

In a Chicago welfare-to-work program providing services to more than 600 women in 1 year, 58% of respondents reported having been victims of domestic violence when they entered the program, and an additional 28% reported such violence in the past. Other welfare-to-work programs in Kansas City, Denver, and Marshalltown, Iowa, reported that from 22% to 69% of their clients had been domestic violence victims (Raphael, 1995). Similarly, 26 workers in several welfare-to-work programs in New York City reported that between 30% and 75% of their clients had been abuse victims and that 25% to 30% of battered women reported losing their jobs because of abuse (Kenney & Brown, 1997; Shepard & Pence, 1988).

These and other disparate studies in large cities and small towns in the West, the East, and the Midwest all indicate that women receiving public assistance are frequently the same women who are victims of domestic violence. Economic dependence is one reason women cite for remaining in abusive relationships. Public assistance has been a way out, at least temporarily, for such women.

Most studies ask welfare clients or their workers how many clients are currently being abused or have been victims of domestic violence in the past. The study described in this chapter examines actual records, rather than relying on opinions of workers or self-reports from clients. Rather than questioning welfare clients about their past or current domestic violence experiences, this study examines data from domestic violence victims who have filed police reports and asks how many of them used welfare and when they applied for it.

If financial obstacles are a major factor that keeps women in abusive relationships, one could logically assume that some of these women might turn to the welfare system to provide an alternative source of financial support in order to escape economic dependence on their abusers. Anecdotally, this was known to occur, but very little independent data support these assumptions and self-reports.

The cited studies document the correlation between family violence and welfare use. What is not known by studying correlations is the temporal relationship between the two events. A correlation alone could be used to argue that those on welfare are more prone to violence, or even that welfare causes the violence. If, however, it could be documented from independent sources that when women have been abused they then turned to welfare, it would lead to the reverse conclusion: that violence leads to the use of welfare. This conclusion has serious implications for the debate on welfare reform.

The Utah Study

A study was conducted in Salt Lake City, the largest city in Utah, with about 40% of the state's population. Utah has a small, stable, fairly homogeneous population. Approximately 75% of the state population is Mormon,[1] with only about 2% African American. The state prides itself on strong family values, self-reliance, and community support for families. The Mormon Church (Church of Jesus Christ of Latter-day Saints) has a strong social service system of its own, separate from the State Department of Human Services. Therefore, whatever relationship exists between domestic violence and the use of welfare might be even stronger in other states with larger, more diverse populations, with fewer family or community support systems available in lieu of the public welfare system.

To look at this relationship, the study compared all domestic violence incident reports[2] from the Salt Lake City Police Department with public assistance benefits records from the Utah Department of Human Services Office of Income Support. Police records were available for 1993, 1994, 1995, and the first 2 months of 1996. Public assistance records were available from 1988 through April 1996.

Because little is known about how domestic violence victims use welfare and under what circumstances, it was necessary to supplement the quantitative data obtained by secondary analysis of these official records with qualitative data obtained from the women themselves. To probe possible explanations for the results found in the records and to obtain questions for further study, focus groups were conducted with residents at a local domestic violence shelter and with women active in JEDI Women (Justice, Economic Dignity, and Independence for Women), a local welfare advocacy organization.

Analysis of Findings: Official Records

Of 3,147 unduplicated reported domestic violence incidents in Salt Lake City from January 1993 to February 1996, between 24% and 31% of women reporting these incidents had sought AFDC. In contrast, AFDC cases represent less than 3% of the state's population.[3] This high proportion of domestic violence cases using welfare is conservative, as not all victims file domestic violence reports.

These figures include both accepted (opened) and denied cases because application indicates intent to use public assistance. That some of those who applied were denied, despite need, is illustrated in the following discussion of focus groups. Possession of a car with a value over $1,500, having one's name listed as co-owner of the family home, or other reasons could disqualify a needy applicant from obtaining assistance.

The high correlation between welfare and family violence (almost one third of all cases), however, does not explain the relationship between these two variables. Some conservative commentators have suggested that families on welfare are prone to violence or even that welfare causes violence, as well as dependence (Murray, 1984). The next set of data refutes such spurious conclusions. To the contrary, it strongly suggests that the violence may lead to the need for welfare.

Date of Incident and Date
Assistance Was Sought

In analyzing the temporal relationship between the date the violent incident occurred and when the AFDC case was opened,[4] we found that between 8.5% and 11.2% of domestic incident cases began to receive AFDC within 6 months after the violent incident and that up to 22% started on AFDC within 1 year after the incident (see Table 4.1).

Although these data cannot definitively prove a causal relationship, the close proximity of the two strongly suggests the scenario that, after the incidents, these women were looking for a way out of the relationships with their abusers and sought public assistance to do so.

Many women who are abused do not file police incident reports, so these figures are conservative. Many women who do not file reports leave their abusers, and presumably some of these women also seek welfare. We have no way of ascertaining how many abused women

Table 4.1 Domestic Violence Victims Using AFDC: 1993-1996 (N = 3147)

	1993 N = 541		1994 N = 429		1995 N = 1,961		1996[a] N = 216	
	#	%	#	%	#	%	#	%
AFDC AS % OF ALL DOMESTIC VIOLENCE (DV) INCIDENTS	125	23.1	101	23.5	525	27.0	61	28
AFDC START AFTER DV INCIDENT:								
Began within 6 months after dv report	14	11.2	11	10.9	45	8.5	2	3.3
Began within 6-12 months after dv report	10	8.0	11	10.9	15	2.8	—	—
TOTAL within 1 year after dv report	24	19.2	22	21.8	60	11.4	2	3.3
Began more than 1 year after dv report	24	19.2	4	3.9	2	0.4	—	—
AFDC START PRIOR TO INCIDENT								
Began within 6 months prior to dv report	14	11.2	11	10.9	75	14.1	10	16.3
Began within 6-12 months prior to dv report	11	8.8	8	7.9	63	12.0	—	—
TOTAL within 1 year prior to dv report	25	20.0	19	18.8	138	26.2	10	16.3
Began more than 1 year prior to dv report	52	41.6	56	55.4	325	61.5	49	80.3
TOTAL began AFDC 1 year prior to/after dv report	49	39.2	41	40.6	198	38.0	10	16.3
AFDC ENDS AFTER DV REPORT								
Ends within 6 months after dv report	4	3.2	9	8.9	103	19.5	12	19.6
Ends 6-12 months after dv report	2	1.6	13	12.8	79	14.9	—	—
TOTAL end within 1 year after dv report	6	4.8	22	21.7	182	34.4	12	19.6
Ends more than 1 year after dv report	51	40.8	30	29.7	19	3.6	—	—
AFDC ENDS BEFORE DV REPORT								
Ends within 6 months prior to dv report	—	—	2	1.9	48	9.1	15	24.5
Ends 6-12 months prior to dv report	2	1.6	3	2.9	23	4.3	3	4.9
TOTAL end AFDC 1 year prior to dv report	2	1.6	5	4.8	71	13.2	18	29.4
Ends more than 1 year prior to dv report	9	7.2	9	8.9	62	11.7	7	11.4
TOTAL end AFDC 1 year prior to/after dv report	8	6.4	27	26.7	253	48.0	30	49.1

NOTE: a. Numbers for 1996 are low because only January and February data were available.

who did not file police reports nevertheless applied for public assistance. Moreover, many earlier domestic violence incidents prior to the one finally reported may have gone unreported. Perhaps the reported incident was the most serious, leading the woman to finally make the break even if it meant having to go on assistance. Or it may mean that, after years of not reporting the abuse, the woman finally gained enough confidence both to report the incident and to finally break away.

Interestingly, and unexpectedly, we also found a similar number of women who began to receive AFDC shortly *before* the domestic violence incident.[5] These data could be used by conservative critics to support the argument that welfare leads to all sorts of family pathology, including domestic violence. Rather, it supports what family violence specialists have observed: Often when the victim attempts to leave she is at greatest risk. According to the U.S. Bureau of Justice Statistics (as cited in New York State Office for Prevention of Domestic Violence, 1993), 75% of domestic violence victims are separated or divorced from their abusers. It is not welfare per se, but the move to independence, that triggers the violence. It is likely that when the women left the abusive relationships and obtained AFDC so that they would no longer have to rely on their abusers for support, the abuse escalated and they finally reported it.

Examining the combined figures of commencement of AFDC within a year before or after the incident report, we found that between 38% and 41% of all those women reporting domestic violence who had used welfare had their AFDC cases opened within 1 year of the reports. Although this fact does not prove causality, it strongly suggests the possibility of such a relationship.

Analysis of Findings: Focus Groups

Focus groups confirmed what had been speculated from the quantitative data reported: Several focus group members said they sought public assistance when they decided to leave their abusers. The type of abuse suffered included physical, sexual, and emotional, alone or in combination. In contrast with popular beliefs that welfare was easy to obtain, many women reported great difficulties and harsh treatment when attempting to obtain assistance.

🔁 Case #1

One young woman, married at 18, had four children and nine pregnancies by age 24, when she separated from her husband after years of marital rape and miscarriages that had left her physically and emotionally damaged. She reported that her husband would deliberately force sex at certain times of the month to get her pregnant, saying, "Now you can't leave me." After she finally sought a divorce, she applied for public assistance, which was a "stressful, demeaning" process. She reported being turned down because her car was above the asset limitation and she was listed as co-owner of her house. With four young children, all infants and toddlers, she did not think she could give up her car. Although home ownership made her ineligible for welfare, she could not afford to pay the mortgage on her house.

Turned down for welfare, she was unable to earn more than minimum wage. Her husband, who had moved back into the family home, convinced her to let him have the children because she was unable to support them. Without the children, she lost any chance of receiving AFDC, and because she left the marriage and the children, the court required her to pay him child support and half the child care costs. Subsequently, he remarried and refused her rights to see the children. She had no money to hire a lawyer to fight him in court. 🔁

🔁 Case #2

Another woman, an observant Mormon, had married at 16, did not finish high school, and had six children. Her husband decided to take multiple wives, and at first she agreed to this arrangement. Subsequently, she found it emotionally agonizing. He became more authoritarian and controlling. She wanted to keep the family together but finally could not bear it and left.

With six children and no work skills, she soon found another man to care for her. She was raised with the belief that the man's role was provider and that the woman's place was in the home, caring for the children. This man became physically abusive, and at the time of the focus group she had recently left him, applying for AFDC.

She expressed concern about the 2-year limit on assistance in the welfare reform bill and requirements that she seek work or education. She believed that her children had been emotionally damaged and that, at least initially, they needed her at home, sometimes "to just hold them." This woman expressed very traditional values: "Men and society need to realize that mothers have a special role and a special gift—just going out to work is not an answer." She later indicated that she wanted her children to be educated before they entered a relationship so that they would be more independent than she was. ᔆ

Several women agreed that it takes time after living for years in an abusive situation until the survivor is able to get out into the world and work. She needs counseling, she must recover her damaged self-esteem, and her children need support. Said one, "You can't focus right after you leave." They feared that the new rules would make it impossible for them and others like them ever to get on their feet.

One woman complained about the "caseworkers" who took applications for welfare. Asked about the provisions of the Wellstone-Murray Family Violence Amendment calling for screening welfare recipients for family violence, she said she was so ashamed of being abused that she would tell no one, least of all an unsympathetic eligibility worker. She was concerned that unless a different kind of caseworker was used, initial screening of clients for domestic violence would be unsuccessful. "She was the last person I would tell I was abused—what makes them think you will admit it—it just doesn't happen."

Women in the shelter who were trying to get jobs expressed difficulties in listing the shelter's address. They found it embarrassing and reported that employers did not like hiring women who lived in a shelter, but they were required to give addresses and could not give their home addresses because their abusers were there. They also complained that the public assistance workers "are trying to get you into the job market . . . but if you're not qualified and they just throw you in . . ." In some states, shelters forbid their residents from working, as stalking abusers could find them, follow them to the shelter, and thus jeopardize the safety of all the residents.

🗿 Case #3

> *Another woman had also married young—at 16—and had*
> *three children by age 20. She had no high school degree and no*
> *skills. Her husband was both physically and emotionally*
> *abusive. She finally left him and applied for public assistance*
> *when she had three children and was pregnant with her fourth.*
> *But because she had grown up believing in motherhood and*
> *her obligation to stay home to care for the children, she soon*
> *remarried. This man stayed home and insisted on her working.*
> *When he was to care for the children so that she could go to*
> *work, he would frequently show up drunk or not show up at*
> *all. She refused to leave them alone or with him in that*
> *condition and was fired from several jobs. This perceived*
> *failure in employment further destroyed her self-esteem.*
>
> *Several women reported contradictory messages from their*
> *husbands: They were tired of supporting the women, they*
> *wanted the women to go to school or get a job, but when they*
> *did, the men were jealous and controlling, feared the women's*
> *growing independence, and sabotaged their efforts.*
>
> *Several women reported chronic physical or mental health*
> *conditions as a result of their abuse that impeded their efforts*
> *to be financially independent. These included bladder infec-*
> *tions, anxiety attacks, insomnia, migraine headaches, and*
> *mental illness causing hospitalization and continuing use of*
> *medication.* 🗿

Policy Implications

The data reported here support and corroborate studies by the
Taylor Institute (Raphael, 1996), the McCormack Institute (Allard
et al., 1997), and others regarding the strong correlation between
family violence and welfare. In addition, the findings support the
hypothesis that not only do abused women use welfare but they
actively seek welfare as a way out of abusive situations. Many welfare
recipients have been abused. They need assistance to leave their
abusers. They are often coping with emotionally disturbed children,

physical or emotional problems, severe loss of self-esteem, and lack of education or experience, which makes it difficult for them to get or keep jobs when they first begin to receive welfare. They will need time, and in many instances a variety of supportive services, to enable them to make a successful transition from welfare to work.

The additional finding that women are vulnerable to attack by their abusers shortly after obtaining public assistance suggests that case management, as well as stronger enforcement of laws against harassment and stalking, are necessary. Policymakers and administrators who implement welfare "reform" need to be aware of the difficulties and danger a new client may be facing. In addition to the other problems described, she may be living in terror. To expect her simply to get a job, put her life in order, and quickly become self-sufficient is to callously ignore reality.

Although the 1996 federal Personal Responsibility and Work Opportunity Reconciliation Act (PRA) mandates a maximum lifetime allotment of 60 months for receipt of welfare, states can opt for less time. Utah has passed legislation for a 3-year limit, Connecticut has passed a limit of 21 months, and Texas has passed a lifetime limit of only 18 months. What will happen if women who were previously on welfare remarry and find themselves in abusive situations? If they have used up their lifetime eligibility, will they be afraid to leave, or will they return to their abusers? What responsibility will our lawmakers take for increased violence? These and other policy implications are addressed more fully in the last chapter.

The PRA also mandates work after 2 years and requires work experience or workfare, in most cases, after only 2 months. From what these women have told us, women escaping long-term abuse may not be mentally, emotionally, or physically capable of working. They may feel torn between these requirements and their responsibilities to mother their emotionally damaged children. And what is the cost to the children of requiring these mothers to work—often in make-work, stigmatizing activities that will not even prepare them for real work? And how will they be able to concentrate on work or keep their jobs if they are being stalked by their abusers?

Many of the women had married young and had little education.[6] Education in U.S. society has traditionally been the way up from poverty, the way to create opportunity. National AFDC figures show a clear inverse correlation between level of education and recidivism: Only 2.9% of women with 1 year of college are on public assistance at any point, as compared with 7.3% with only a high school diploma (Shea, 1992). An associate's degree raises a woman's income 65% above that of a woman with a high school diploma. Of women on AFDC who completed just 1 year of college, 75% left voluntarily after 2 years (Kates, n.d.). Yet, the PRA does not recognize post-high school education as a work activity (with the exception of up to 1 year of vocational education for a maximum of 20% of the caseload).

Nationally, women on welfare have an average of 1.8 children. In Utah, families are larger. The more children a woman has, the more difficult it is to afford child care and become self-supporting, particularly without educational preparation. Without further education, many women will be consigned to depend on men, even abusive ones, to support them and their children. Yet, the new law severely limits education and training in favor of immediate work, often in low-paying, dead-end jobs or in workfare, without any benefits or opportunity for advancement into real jobs.

As described in Chapter 1, the Family Violence Amendment, optional for states, calls for the screening of all federally funded public assistance (Temporary Assistance for Needy Families, or TANF) applicants and recipients for domestic violence; referral of victims of domestic violence for appropriate services and counseling; and the waiving of time limits, family caps, child support reporting, and other provisions of the law when these might further jeopardize or penalize the women.

As important as adopting the amendment is,[7] how it is implemented is the key to its success or failure. As one recipient indicated, many women simply will not admit to a harried, unfriendly public assistance worker that she is a victim of abuse. It is imperative that caseworkers who are trained in interviewing, skilled in listening, and knowledgeable about domestic violence be employed. Adequate numbers of staff will be necessary as well to provide an individualized plan for appropriate services and waivers. Both quality and quantity of staff are necessary for successful implementation. If an agency's goal is merely to reduce the number of recipients receiving public assistance, there will be little incentive to identify all those in need or to provide appropriate service and extend time limits.

Conclusions

There is little doubt that the use of welfare is inextricably linked with domestic violence. Growing evidence, as reported in this study, suggests that women seek public assistance to leave abusive situations. Evidence also suggests that women who seek assistance as a way of becoming independent of their abusers are at risk of further violence. The Family Violence Option can help protect some of these women against the harshest provisions of the new federal welfare reform law.

It is essential that all those working with welfare applicants and recipients understand the dynamics of abusive relationships. Rather than simply attempt to reduce the welfare rolls as quickly as possible, welfare workers need to develop plans with their clients to ensure their safety, provide realistic expectations and appropriate supports that will protect their safety, and help them eventually become financially independent.

Similarly, those working with domestic violence victims need to understand the welfare system, advocate for appropriate services and exemptions as provided for under the Wellstone-Murray Amendment, and provide safety plans for those seeking public assistance as well as employment.

If the public can begin to understand the humanity of individual welfare recipients, perhaps we can begin to move from a punitive to a caring welfare system.

Notes

1. Salt Lake City, by far the largest city in the state, has a population that is approximately 50% Mormon, whereas the rest of the state is about 90% Mormon.

2. These reports dated from January 1993, when this information began to be collected systematically, through February 1996, the latest data available at the time of the study.

3. In this chapter, only AFDC findings are discussed. A few cases applied for or received general assistance or food stamps only. Both of these are alternative sources of public assistance; the former is a cash grant for those ineligible for AFDC, the latter is an in-kind food voucher. Application for either indicates an attempt to seek financial support. Although the figures were too small to merit analysis here, the patterns were similar to those described for AFDC.

4. In analyzing these data, only those actually receiving AFDC were included. Because only 2 months were available for 1996, analysis was not done for this period as it would have been skewed.

5. Between 11% and 14% began to receive assistance 6 months before the domestic violence incident, and between 19% and 26% within 1 year before.

6. National figures indicate that 50% of those on AFDC do not have a high school degree; another 45% have only a high school degree.

7. By September 1997, according to the NOW Legal Defense and Educational Fund, 28 states had adopted the amendment and another 18 have some domestic violence language or provisions in their plans.

References

Allard, M. A., Colten, M. E., Albelda, R., & Cosenza, C. (1997). *In harm's way? Domestic violence, AFDC receipt, and welfare reform in Massachusetts.* Boston: University of Massachusetts, McCormack Institute, Center for Survey Research.

Ellwood, D. (1988). *Poor support: Poverty in the American family.* New York: Basic Books.

Gilder, G. (1981). *Wealth and poverty.* New York: Basic Books.

Kates, E. (n.d.). *Getting smart about welfare.* Washington, DC: Center for Women's Policy Studies.

Kaus, M. (1992). *The end of equality.* New York: Basic Books.

Kenney, C., & Brown, K. (1997). *Report from the front lines: The impact of violence on poor women.* New York: NOW Legal Defense and Education Fund.

Murray, C. (1984). *Losing ground: American social policy, 1950-1980.* New York: Basic Books.

New York State Office for the Prevention of Domestic Violence. (1993, July). *Domestic violence fact sheet.* Rensselaer: Author.

Raphael, J. (1995). *Domestic violence: Telling the untold welfare-to-work story.* Chicago: Taylor Institute.

Raphael, J. (1996). *Prisoners of abuse: Domestic violence and welfare receipt.* Chicago: Taylor Institute.

Shea, M. (1992). *Characteristics of recipients and the dynamics of program participation, 1987-1988.* Washington, DC: U.S. Bureau of the Census.

Shepard, M., & Pence, E. (1988). The effect of battering on the employment status of women. *Affilia, 3*(2), 55-61.

University of Utah Survey Research Center. (1993, November). *Self-sufficiency needs assessment for single parents receiving AFDC.* Salt Lake City: Author.

Washington State Institute for Public Policy. (1993, October). *Family income study.* Olympia: Author.

5

Pursuing Child
Support for Victims
of Domestic Violence

Paula Roberts

Victims of domestic violence often seek public assistance to escape from and/or remain free of this violence. To be eligible for cash assistance, however, a mother must *assign* her child support rights to the state. Unless she can claim an exemption, she must also *cooperate* with the state in establishing paternity (if that is an issue), obtaining a support order, and enforcing that order. Unfortunately, the pursuit of child support can—and often does—engender more violence (Allard, Colten, Albelda, & Cosenza, 1997; Pearson & Griswold, 1997). Recently enacted federal legislation may help address this problem. The legislation also has the potential to make the problem worse. The outcome will largely depend on what policies individual states adopt in implementing the new federal welfare legislation.

To help concerned citizens understand and develop positions on the issues, this chapter begins by describing the child support assignment and cooperation requirements that domestic violence victims had to face under the Aid to Families With Dependent Children (AFDC) program. Then it delineates the child support provisions contained in the recently enacted Personal Responsibility and Work Opportunity Reconciliation Act (PRA) of 1996. Finally, it offers some suggestions for how to approach the issues raised by the new law.

Before doing so, however, it is helpful to put the child support issue in context. The vast majority of children who live with only one of their parents live with their mother. Women still face a job market that offers lower wages and fewer opportunities than are available to men. The result is that most single-parent families headed by women live below, at, or only slightly above the poverty line (Lino, 1996). These families need child support to supplement the mothers' earnings. Data from the U.S. Bureau of the Census (1995) underscore this point: In 1992, the mean annual income of mother-only families that received regular child support was $18,144; the mean income of those who had a child support order but did not actually receive payments was $14,602; and similar families without even a support order had a mean annual income of $10,226. Clearly, child support can make a difference in the ability of mothers to house, feed, and clothe their children.

As the country moves into a welfare system where help is available only on a time-limited basis, child support payments become even more important. Mothers leaving welfare for low-wage jobs will *need* child support payments to survive. Mothers whose families have "used up" their eligibility for time-limited public assistance may have only child support to fall back on.

These harsh realities affect all low-income mothers, especially those who need public assistance. When these mothers are also domestic violence victims, the realities are even harsher. Domestic violence victims need time to recover physically and psychologically from their abuse. They may face problems getting and keeping jobs if their partners sabotage their work efforts or stalk them at work (Raphael, 1996). If these women are not able to obtain exemptions from time limits or work requirements imposed by the new welfare law, many will have no public assistance to rely on. Their only available alternative may be to return to abusive relationships.

Moreover, failure to collect child support rewards perpetrators of violence by relieving them of financial responsibility for their children. Indeed, many women see fathers' refusal to meet their child support obligations as a continuation of the intimidation that is part of a pattern of violence. They want to pursue child support if they can do so safely.

Therein lies the fundamental dilemma. Is it possible to pursue the child support income that domestic violence victims need and still keep them and their children safe? To date, the child support system has avoided dealing with this issue. It has never tried to establish mechanisms in which support is pursued but domestic violence victims are protected from their abusers. In implementing the new welfare reform law, the issues can no longer be avoided. Thought has to be given to the development of a system in which mothers can pursue child support and be free of retaliatory violence. Failure to come to grips with the problem will leave many families with no income source (when their eligibility for public assistance ceases) and force others to return to abusive relationships because public assistance is no longer an option.

Assignment and Cooperation
in the AFDC System

To understand the decisions that states will be making, it is helpful to start with the relationship between cash assistance and the pursuit of child support under the old federal law, specifically Title IVA of the Social Security Act (42 U.S.C. § 602[a][26], 1975). This analysis is helpful both as background and because it identifies potential problems that need to be addressed in implementing the new law. The old law contained three distinct concepts. The first concept was *assignment*. As a condition of eligibility, a mother applying for or receiving AFDC had to assign her right to collect child support to the state. This was nonnegotiable. The state then used the assignment as the basis of its claim to pursue (or its refusal to pursue) child support.

The second concept was *cooperation*. Under the old law, the mother was required to cooperate with the state child support enforcement (IVD) agency in locating the father, establishing paternity, obtaining and periodically modifying the support order, and enforcing that order. Like assignment, this was an eligibility condition for receiving AFDC. If a mother failed to cooperate, her needs were removed from the AFDC grant, and the assistance payment went (if possible) to a protective payee on behalf of the child(ren). Federal regulations (Code of Federal Regulations, 45 CFR § 232.12, 1996) defined *cooperation* to include (a) providing whatever information the mother had or attesting to a lack of information, (b) attending conferences at the child support agency, (c) submitting herself and the child to genetic tests if such tests were ordered by a court or administrative agency, (d) appearing at any court/administrative agency hearings, and (e) turning over to the state any child support payments received directly from the father.

All of this was supposed to be explained to the mother at the time she applied for AFDC. At that time, the AFDC worker was also supposed to explain the third concept of the system, the *good cause exception.*

The Good Cause Exception

The federal regulations (45 CFR § 232.40, 1996) provided four possible reasons why a mother might claim a good cause exception from cooperating with the state in pursuing support: (a) Pursuing support was reasonably anticipated to result in physical or emotional harm to the mother or the child, (b) the child was conceived as the result of forcible rape or incest, (c) adoption proceedings were pending, or (d) the mother was working with a social worker to determine whether the child should be placed for adoption.

Written notice about the availability of the good cause exception to the cooperation requirement was supposed to be given to the mother *before* requiring her cooperation. At state option, this could have been done in one of two ways: (a) Give the mother one long notice providing all required information, or (b) provide her with an initial notice containing basic information and alerting her to the existence of the good cause exception followed by a second notice (if she indicated she might wish to claim good cause) containing more detailed information about how to make a good cause claim. The notice(s) had to cover the following:

- Why it was a good thing to pursue child support
- What the cooperation requirement (described above) was
- That cooperation in pursuing child support was an eligibility condition for obtaining cash assistance
- That there was a good cause exception to the cooperation requirement and what it entailed
- What corroborative information was required in order to make a good cause claim and that (if needed) the agency would assist in obtaining such information

- That if a good cause claim was made, the agency would investigate the claim and make a judgment based on the evidence
- That the standard for judging a claim of good cause was the "best interests of the child"
- That refusal to cooperate without good cause would result in a grant reduction

To document the fact that notice was actually given, federal regulations required that the case file contain a signed and dated acknowledgment by the mother and the caseworker that she had received such a notice. Moreover, the mother was to be given a copy of the notice for future reference.

Another set of federal regulations (45 CFR § 232.43, 1996) set out what the mother had to prove in order to establish a good cause claim. Under these regulations, a domestic violence claim was not easy to prove. *Official records* had to be somewhere in the system in order to establish a case. Without law enforcement, court, medical, child protective services, or social services records, it was impossible to make a successful claim. Moreover, if the mother could not produce such documents, the state could contact the father and ask him to corroborate the mother's claim of abuse! If the mother could produce sufficient evidence, however, the AFDC program would excuse her from cooperation, and child support would not be pursued.[1]

Social science research and case law documented some problems with this system. One was that the AFDC workers did a very poor job of interviewing mothers and of getting information about the fathers (General Accounting Office, 1987). Another was that AFDC caseworkers did a poor job of explaining, or neglected to meet their obligation to explain to their clients either the cooperation requirement or the good cause exception (Roberts & Finkel, 1994). Typically, the required written notice about the cooperation requirement and the good cause exception was part of a lengthy package of forms the mother was asked to sign. She would sign the form without having the time to read it or digest its contents. This left mothers unclear about their cooperation obligation and unsure how to raise concerns about domestic violence. A third criticism of the old system was that the standards for proving a good cause claim were so high that few domestic violence victims could meet them (Johnson & Blong, 1987).

In any case, a clear discrepancy existed between the number of domestic violence cases and the number of women who ever claimed a good cause exception from the cooperation requirement. For example, in 1995, only 8,387 good cause claims were made in the entire country. Colorado, Delaware, Iowa, Kansas, Maryland, and Nebraska reported no claims at all. Alaska, Hawaii, Louisiana, Maine, Minnesota, Nevada, New Mexico, South Dakota, Texas, and Utah reported fewer than 50 such claims in the entire year (U.S. Office of Child Support Enforcement, 1997). These data are clearly at odds with the emerging information about the frequency of domestic violence among mothers receiving public assistance (Salomon, Bassuk, & Brooks, 1996).

One possible explanation for this inconsistency is that domestic violence victims who had legitimate fears about retaliation if they pursued child support may have been using the provision of the regulations that allowed them to attest to a lack of information about the fathers or their whereabouts in order to avoid pursuing support. AFDC workers—faced with mothers who had legitimate fears of domestic violence but no way to prove a case under the regulations—may also have been implicitly or explicitly suggesting to their clients that the best thing for them to do was simply to say they didn't have much information. This answer allowed the mothers to avoid the fathers' wrath and the risk of a breach of confidentiality about their whereabouts. It also allowed the AFDC workers to avoid putting the effort into establishing a good cause case (Johnson & Blong, 1987). In the end, it thwarted the pursuit of support and denied mothers access to the very financial resources they may have needed in order to avoid returning to abusive relationships. It also allowed the child support system to avoid determining how to set up a system that both collects the needed support and protects the client from violence.

The Personal Responsibility and Work Opportunity Reconciliation Act of 1996

As discussed in Chapter 1, the Personal Responsibility and Work Opportunity Reconciliation Act of 1996 (PRA) abolished the AFDC program and replaced it in Title I with a new program called Temporary Assistance for Needy Families (TANF). The new law is supposed to give states more flexibility in designing public assistance programs. For that reason, it contains federal standards but let the states make choices in some major areas. In the child support area, the new law retains a federal requirement that those receiving assistance assign their support rights to the state (PRA, 42 U.S.C. § 608[a][3], 1996). It also retains some federal guidance on "cooperation" and "good cause" exceptions to the cooperation requirement. States, however, are given new discretion in some areas (42 U.S.C. § 654[29]):

Cooperation

- The federal statute defines cooperation to include making a good faith effort to provide the state with information about the noncustodial parent; appearing at interviews, hearings, and legal proceedings; and submitting oneself and one's child(ren) to genetic tests, if needed.
- States are free to supplement these federal standards with their own standards, particularly in regard to how much information about the father the mother seeking public assistance must provide. The only federal guidance is that the standard must include a good faith effort to provide his name and such other identifying information that the state decides is appropriate.
- Federal law sets the minimum penalty for failure to cooperate without good cause at a 25% reduction in the family's TANF grant. States are free to adopt even harsher sanctions up to and including the denial of TANF assistance to the entire family.

Good Cause

- States are free to develop their own ideas about, and standards for, proving any good cause exceptions to the cooperation requirement.
- States are also free to develop "other exceptions" to the cooperation requirement as they see fit.
- The only federal constraint is that such definitions must be based on "the best interests of the child."

Implementation Procedures

The federal law also sets up a process for making these determinations. Under that law, the *child support agency,* rather than the public assistance agency, must be responsible for making the cooperation determination. If the agency determines that a mother is not cooperating, it must promptly notify her and the TANF agency of the determination (PRA, 42 U.S.C. § 654[29][E], 1996). The TANF agency must then sanction the mother, imposing whatever penalty the state has chosen. This can range from the minimum 25% reduction in assistance to the denial of assistance to the entire family. If the TANF agency does not enforce the penalties requested by the child support agency, then the federal government can reduce the state's TANF funds by up to 5% (PRA, 42 U.S.C. § 609[a][5]).

While requiring that the cooperation determination be made by the child support agency, the federal statute gives the TANF agency the right to make the good cause determination. (If the family receives Medicaid, the Medicaid agency may make a separate good cause determination.)

Missing from the federal scheme is any mention of notice to families about either the cooperation requirement or the good cause exceptions. Also missing are any mention of the standards (aside from the rather vague "best interests of the child") for establishing exceptions; any allusion to the standards of proof or kind of process to be used in making either cooperation or good cause determinations; and any guidance on coordination of activities between the IUD agency's cooperation decisions and the TANF agency's good cause decisions.

This leaves states with the obligation to (a) define "cooperation in good faith"; (b) develop definitions of "good cause" and "other exceptions" to the cooperation requirement; (c) promulgate standards for proving a "good cause" or "other exceptions" claim; (d) establish protocols for coordination between agencies if more than one is to be involved; (e) design due process notice and hearing procedures for administering the requirements; and (f) determine what sanction (if any) beyond the federal minimum should be applied.

In doing this, states can take advantage of a provision in the law (the Wellstone-Murray Amendment, or the Family Violence Option) that allows them to give special consideration to families in which domestic violence has occurred (PRA, 42 U.S.C. § 602[a][7]). Under it, in developing their TANF implementation plans, states can indicate that they will screen cases for domestic violence issues and protect the confidentiality of individuals who have been battered and that they will refer affected families to counseling and support services. In addition, if a state chooses this route, it can waive TANF program requirements, including time limits, work requirements, and child support cooperation if there is good cause to do so.

The new federal law also provides a definition of "domestic violence" (PRA, 42 U.S.C. § 608[a][7][C][iii]) that is fully described in the last chapter of this book. Before leaving this description of the new law, three other points need to be mentioned.[2]

Child Support and Food Stamps

Until now, some battered mothers could avoid the child support cooperation dilemma by seeking noncash assistance, particularly food stamps. Because there was no child support cooperation policy within the Food Stamp Program, these mothers did not have to face the cooperation/good cause issues. The new federal law, however, gives states the *option* to impose a child support cooperation requirement on custodial parents seeking or receiving food stamps (PRA, 7 U.S.C. § 2015[l]). Failure to meet this obligation, unless there is "good cause," makes the custodial parent ineligible for assistance from the program. The Secretary of Agriculture is to issue regulations establishing standards for the good cause exceptions. States that exercise this option will have to implement cooperation and good cause exception policies. Domestic violence victims in those states will then face the same dilemma in the Food Stamp Program as they do in the cash assistance area.

Child Support and Medicaid

For the last several years, a child support cooperation requirement has existed (with a good cause exception) in Medicaid (Social Security Act, Title XIX, 42 U.S.C. § 1396k [a][1], 1988). This remains in place under the welfare reform law. In the past, this was not of particular concern to mothers receiving cash assistance because eligibility for Medicaid was linked with AFDC eligibility, and satisfaction of the AFDC cooperation requirement was almost always considered satisfaction of the Medicaid cooperation requirement (Roberts, 1992). An attestation of a lack of knowledge about the father or his whereabouts that was accepted by the AFDC system would be enough for eligibility under Medicaid. A determination of "good cause" by the AFDC system was rarely challenged by Medicaid. Under the new law, however, Medicaid and cash assistance are decoupled. As a result, the child support agency will be administering Medicaid cooperation requirements while the Medicaid agency will be making good cause determinations. The Medicaid agency's good cause determination will be made separately from the TANF agency's good cause determination for purposes of cash assistance. This raises the possibility of conflicting rules and procedures between the agencies and confusion for the mothers. The result could be the denial of much-needed medical care.

Child Support and Supplemental Security Income

In recent years, the Supplemental Security Income (SSI) program (which provides benefits to people with disabilities) has expanded to cover children who have emotional and behavioral problems. Many of these children have the types of disabilities likely to be experienced by those who have been the victims of abuse or who have witnessed domestic violence involving other family members. Indeed, both anecdotal and research evidence indicate that abused women are significantly more likely to have children with ongoing disabilities than are nonabused women (Allard et al., 1997). The SSI program has no child support cooperation requirement, so the problem of whether to pursue child support for these children has largely been left up to the mother. She could apply to the state child support agency for assistance in establishing paternity and pursuing support if she wished. If, in her judgment, this was not desirable because of domestic violence concerns, she did not have to seek child support.

For some SSI families, this will now change. Some children with disabilities will lose their SSI benefits because of the federal law's strict new definition of disability. Their families will then likely apply for TANF assistance. At this point, their mothers will have to cooperate in pursuing child support unless they qualify for a good cause exception under the rules described above. These cases will need special handling by the child support agency. Both the mothers and the children may need to be protected.

Possible Approaches to These Changes

Victims of domestic violence and those concerned about them can use this time of change to improve the system in their state and ensure that domestic violence victims receive the help they need. A good starting place is advocating adoption of the Family Violence Option described above. The advantages of adopting the Family Violence Option approach include the following:

- Open recognition by the state of the need to develop standards and procedures for dealing with families for whom domestic violence is an issue
- The possibility for early identification (at either application or recertification) of families for whom domestic violence is a problem
- Use of a broad federal definition that categorizes physical and mental abuse, as well as inappropriate sexual behavior, directed against mothers and/or their children as "domestic violence"
- Acknowledgment of the usefulness of providing counseling and supportive services to families so that they can permanently escape the violence and rebuild their lives
- Mandatory attention to confidentiality issues
- Consistent treatment of families so that those with a need for a good cause exception to any TANF requirement are dealing with trained caseworkers who are all using the same set of rules

Depending on the state, adoption of the Family Violence Option could be done through state legislation[3] or through executive branch action.

Another decision that might be made by either the legislature or the governor is whether to pursue the Food Stamp Program child support cooperation option. This option allows the state to impose a child support cooperation requirement (subject to good cause exceptions) on custodial parents receiving food stamps. For families in the TANF program who also receive food stamps, the imposition of a separately administered food stamp child support cooperation requirement would be redundant. It would also raise the possibility that the Food Stamp Program would have different standards for good cause than the TANF program has because the Food Stamp Program rules would be set out by the U.S. secretary of agriculture, whereas the TANF rules will be determined by each state.

For families receiving food stamps but not receiving TANF, a cooperation requirement poses a different issue. If the custodial parent wants to pursue support, she is free to do so simply by applying for services from the state child support enforcement agency. If she does not wish to do so, she does not have to seek such services. Given the economic needs of families receiving food stamps, it is highly unlikely that a mother would not pursue child support. The most likely reasons that she would not seek support are a lack of knowledge that services were available, an inability to pay any state-imposed fees, and a fear of domestic violence. Thus, states that exercise the food stamp child support cooperation requirement would end up unnecessarily duplicating the cooperation requirement for TANF families, wasting public resources in the process. They would also bring a group of people into the child support system who have a high likelihood of making a good cause claim. Again, this would be a waste of resources. A more cost-effective approach for states wishing to pursue aggressively child support for families receiving food stamps would be an outreach campaign to non-TANF food stamp households to be sure they know that child support enforcement services are available to them. This should be coupled with a waiver of any fees for those households wishing to pursue child support enforcement services.

The other major decision a state must make is what sanction to impose on TANF households found to be non-cooperating. The federal law states that the minimum penalty must be a 25% grant reduction. States can and should stop there. Given the need for child support income in the time-limited TANF world, there is little reason for mothers not to cooperate with the child support enforcement system. If they are not doing so, it is likely that a reason—such as domestic violence that they are not able to acknowledge—is behind their actions. Punishing them and their children by even harsher sanctions is not likely to bring about cooperation and is likely to harm the children.

Advocacy for adoption of the Family Violence Option and the minimum sanction policy and against the Food Stamp Program option is only a starting point, however. In some states, adoption of these approaches is not politically possible. In others, the states will adopt these approaches but will still need help in fleshing out the specifics. In this regard, in the area of child support enforcement, several clusters of issues must be considered: (a) informing women about the child support system and its cooperation requirements and good cause exceptions in a clear fashion, (b) creating protections within the child support system for those who wish to pursue child support but do not wish to endanger themselves or their children, (c) developing cooperation and good cause standards and provisions that encourage women to think through their options, and (d) implementing and administering both cooperation and good cause provisions in a humane and coherent way. Below is the outline of an approach to these issues:

**Informing Women About the Child
Support System and Its Cooperation
Requirements and Good Cause Exceptions**

As noted above, one major problem in the AFDC system was the failure to explain clearly to mothers what the child support cooperation requirement was and what the good cause exceptions were. The only information a mother might receive was a written notice contained in a pile of other notices she was being asked to sign. The new TANF system should address this problem by providing a variety of forms of notice in a variety of settings. To accomplish this:

1. Simple, clear and coherent materials need to be developed explaining what the TANF child support enforcement system is and how it works. These materials should explain the "cooperation" obligation and "good cause" exceptions. They should also explain what protections the state can offer to women who have been abused but do wish to pursue support.

2. These materials should include videos, as well as written materials, that are in whatever languages are spoken in the community and, if written, at the appropriate reading level.

3. Written and visual materials should be made available at the TANF office and throughout the community. Special attention should be paid to making materials available at social services agencies, WIC clinics, and doctors' offices, particularly to providers offering services to domestic violence victims and battered women's shelters.

4. All TANF intake and recertification workers should receive basic training in identifying and discussing domestic violence issues with applicants and recipients. If possible, a private space should be available in TANF offices where mothers can speak freely and confidentially once the problem has been identified.

5. A copy of the written notice of the good cause and cooperation provisions, signed both by the client and the worker, should be included in the case file and a copy given to the mother for future reference. Mothers should receive new copies of these materials periodically or at any point in the process that it appears domestic violence may be a problem.

6. If the state does decide to opt for a Food Stamp Program child support cooperation requirement for custodial parents, then integra-

tion of that fact, and information about any differences between the TANF and Food Stamp Program standards and procedures, should be covered in the available materials.

Creating Protections for Those Who Wish to Pursue Child Support

To make an informed decision about whether to seek a good cause exception, a mother who has been the victim of domestic violence needs to know about the kinds of protections the system can offer to her if she does wish to pursue child support. Her only choice should not be to invoke a good cause exception and forego support. She should also have the option of going after the support if she can do so safely.

To make this possible, states will have to adopt policies that protect her confidentiality and that minimize or eliminate any face-to-face contact between the mother or child involved and the abuser. They will also have to train staff to be sensitive to the family's concerns and create a system that has the flexibility to stop pursuing support quickly if the violence recurs and there is no way to protect the victims. To this end, the following steps should be taken:

1. All cases involving domestic violence issues should be specially coded and computer flagged within the system. Information about the case, any available documentation, and a statement of whether a protective order was issued and the terms and conditions of the order should be entered into the file.

2. If the mother does not have a protective order and she wishes to obtain one, the system should have the capacity to refer her to an entity (e.g., court, legal services, states attorney, pro se program) that can help her do so.

3. Information about the location of the mother and child(ren) should be protected from disclosure. This can be done in a variety of ways, but one particularly worthy of note is the use of a dummy address. One model here is the Address Confidentiality Program (ACP), which operates in the state of Washington (Address Confidentiality for Victims of Domestic Violence, Revised Code, 1991). In this program, the Secretary of State serves as the battered mother's legal agent for receipt of mail and service of process, and she receives a

substitute address. She then uses the substitute address—not her actual address—in official documents. Thus, if someone inadvertently discloses the address to the batterer, it will do him no good.

4. The protections offered by this system should be explained to the mother during the TANF intake/recertification interview so that she can assess whether they offer sufficient protection to make it feasible to pursue support. All cases in which good cause is claimed should be periodically reevaluated to determine whether the situation has changed and the mother now thinks it would be safe to proceed with a child support action.

5. If the mother wishes to proceed, she should be informed every time a step is taken on the case (e.g., papers are served, an interview is scheduled). Thus, she will know that the batterer may be rankled, and she should take special precautions.

6. If court or agency appearances are scheduled, the mother should be required to attend only if absolutely necessary. If this is the case, she should be afforded protection, she and the batterer should never be left alone, and each should leave the building at a different time and from a different exit.

7. If a visitation order is in place, then arrangements for pick-up and drop-off of the child by a third party at a neutral location need to be provided. If advisable, a motion to preclude visitation or to provide for supervised visitation should also be sought. In the vast majority of states, payment of child support and visitation are legally separate issues; a parent's obligation to pay support is not dependent on having visitation rights with the child.

8. At any point where it appears that the system cannot protect the family, prosecution of the support case should cease.

9. If the state chooses to implement the Food Stamp Program child support cooperation requirement, similar steps should be taken in that program so that the mother can be protected.

Developing Cooperation and Good
Cause Standards and Procedures

Even with a good system of protections in place, some mothers will decide that the risk to themselves or their children is still too great. These mothers will wish to claim a good cause exception to the cooperation requirement. They will then have to deal with the system the state has developed for making cooperation and good cause determinations.

Every state will develop a definition of cooperation for purposes of child support enforcement obligations. As noted above, this will include the state's deciding how much and what kind of information must be provided to meet the threshold requirement. Every state must also develop a definition of good cause or other exceptions that will excuse a mother from meeting the cooperation requirement. Once these definitions are in place, the state will also have to decide what standards will be used for deciding whether a legitimate good cause claim has been presented. Suggestions in this area include the following:

1. *Before* any information about the noncustodial parent is solicited, the caseworker should provide the mother with the materials described above, determine whether a potential domestic violence issue is involved, and explain the protections the system can offer. The abuser's name and other information about him should be obtained only *after* the mother has made the decision that it is safe to proceed.

2. States should adopt the AFDC cooperation regulations as the cooperation standard in their new TANF programs. AFDC regulations contained a definition of cooperation that seems to have worked fairly well. Rather than strict listings of specific information required, it allowed the mother to present all the information she had. The federal AFDC regulations also acknowledged that some mothers have little or no information about the missing fathers. A mother who was raped, for example, may not know the identity of her attacker. A mother who fled a violent relationship several years ago may have old information about the father of her child but have no current information other than his name. In those cases, the mother could attest to her lack of information, and this would be sufficient to meet the cooperation requirement.

3. States should adopt enhanced versions of the federal AFDC regulations defining good cause. AFDC regulations acknowledged that families in which the mother and/or the child(ren) had been victims of domestic violence and those in which the child had been conceived as a result of rape or incest might have good cause for not pursuing child support. These old federal regulations are a good starting place for states in developing their own TANF good cause exceptions to the cooperation requirement. In addition to these, states might consider granting good cause or other exceptions in situations

where it may not be good for the children to have contact with the noncustodial parent because of a history of drug dealing, alcohol abuse, or violence toward nonfamily members. Also, if there is reason to believe that a noncustodial parent would pursue a custody or visitation action to harass the custodial parent for seeking child support, an exception to the cooperation requirement ought to be available.

4. States should establish new standards of evidence for proving a good cause claim. Although listings of acceptable evidence for proving a good cause claim existed under the old federal regulations, they are not necessarily a good place to start because they required official corroboration of the allegation of abuse and such corroboration is not always available. In developing standards for evidence in the TANF program, states need to go beyond formal documents and look at other forms of evidence. These evidence requirements can best be developed in conjunction with experts in domestic violence (including the mothers themselves) to reflect realistic requirements that can be met in typical domestic violence cases. Special attention needs to be paid to situations where the victim has no official documentation. Residence in a shelter or safe house ought to be presumptive evidence. Affidavits from the victim herself and from any witnesses should be acceptable when other proof is not available. Unless a state has independent evidence that a woman is not telling the truth, a declaration from the woman herself should be sufficient.

5. A basic standard of proof for a good cause or other exceptions claim also needs to be decided. The standard should be a "preponderance of the evidence."

6. Caseworkers should have an affirmative obligation to assist domestic violence victims wishing to assert a good cause claim to obtain available evidence and fill out affidavits.

7. If the state invokes the Food Stamp cooperation option, to the maximum extent feasible the process and procedure for that obligation should be made consistent with the TANF standards and procedures.

Implementing and Administering the Good Cause
Provisions in a Humane and Coherent Way

As noted above, the federal statute requires that the child support cooperation determination be made by the child support agency.

Responsibility for the good cause determination, however, is given to the TANF agency.

It can be argued that, for the sake of simplicity, both determinations should be made by the same agency. The system would be streamlined and internally consistent. In addition, a mother would have to deal with only one worker, and it would be clear who had responsibility for explaining the system to the mother.

However, there is some advantage to making the TANF agency responsible for good cause determinations. The TANF agency can do an initial screen for domestic violence and, if this might be an issue, it can assist in developing the good cause claim. If one is found, the case would stop there and never be referred to the child support agency. The advantage of this approach is that it screens out cases in which child support should not be pursued *before* they get to the child support agency. If the child support agency never gets a case, there is no possibility of a later dispute about cooperation. This model also has the advantage of limiting the number of places in which information about the mother and her children is available. For those hiding from abusers, this can be a real consideration. The more systems collecting information such as an address, the greater the chance that the information will become available either as a public record or inadvertently.

This bifurcated approach is particularly sensible in states implementing the Family Violence Option. If the state chooses this approach (or some variation on it), then the TANF agency will be actively screening for domestic violence issues and will be making good cause exceptions for a variety of program purposes (e.g., whether time limits or residency requirements should apply to the family). In that case, it seems obvious that the child support good cause determination should be integrated into this larger process and thus the TANF agency should make the determination.

If the state is not going to provide special consideration to domestic violence victims, then the state must set up protocols to assure consistency between the agency making the cooperation determination and the agency determining good cause.

In any case, the following could be incorporated into any state protocols:

1. If domestic violence issues are involved, the case should be transferred to a specially trained worker or unit (depending on the

size of the office). That worker should examine the situation with the mother and determine whether child support should be pursued, a protective order should be sought (if one is not already in place), or a good cause exception claimed.

2. If a good cause exception is to be pursued, no referral should be made to the child support enforcement agency until the good cause claim had been adjudicated and any appeals finalized.

3. The caseworker (be it in TANF or the child support agency) should start with the premise that child support should be pursued whenever it is possible to do so and still protect the family. The importance of collecting support, what protections can be offered, and how the mother can help should be explored.

Although not perfect, this set of procedures recognizes the competing concerns of securing support for children and protecting families that have experienced physical or psychological violence. It attempts to balance those competing concerns within a system that focuses on creating the kinds of protections needed by victims of such violence so that they can obtain the financial resources they need to avoid returning to the batterer.

Notes

1. Technically, on the basis of the assignment discussed above, the child support agency could decide to pursue support without her cooperation. This was rarely done, however.

2. The law also raises concerns about the availability of assistance to legal immigrants who have been battered. A discussion of those issues is beyond the scope of this chapter.

3. The NOW Legal Defense and Education Fund has developed model language for a state statute. This is part of their Family Violence Option Packet and is available by contacting Diane Greenhals, at NOW Legal Defense and Education Fund, 119 Constitution Avenue NE, Washington, DC 20002.

References

Address Confidentiality for Victims of Domestic Violence, Revised Code of Washington State, Chapter 40.24 (1991).

Allard, M. A., Colten, M. E., Albelda, R., & Cosenza, C. (1997). *In harm's way? Domestic violence, AFDC receipt, and welfare reform in Massachusetts.* Boston: University of Massachusetts, McCormack Institute, Center for Survey Research.

Code of Federal Regulations, (CFR) 45 (1996).

General Accounting Office. (1987). *Child support: Need to improve efforts to identify fathers and obtain support orders* (GAO-HRD-87-37). Washington, DC: Government Printing Office.

Johnson, J., & Blong, A. (1987). The AFDC child support cooperation requirement, *Clearinghouse Review, 21,* 1389-1409.

Lino, M. (1996). Expenditures on children by families, 1995. *Family Economics and Nutrition Review, 9,* 2-20.

Pearson, J., & Griswold, E. (1997, February). *Child support policies and domestic violence.* Paper presented at the Cooperation/Good Cause Forum sponsored by the Federal Office of Child Support Enforcement, Washington, DC.

Personal Responsibility and Work Opportunity Reconciliation Act of 1996, Pub. L. 104-193, 110 Stat. 2105 (August 22, 1996).

Raphael, J. (1996). *Prisoners of abuse: Domestic violence and welfare receipt.* Chicago: Taylor Institute.

Roberts, P. (1992). Cooperation in pursuit of medical support as an eligibility condition for AFDC and Medicaid. *Clearinghouse Review, 26,* 295-301.

Roberts, P., & Finkel, J. (1994). *Establishing paternity for AFDC children: What's right and what's wrong with the current system.* Washington, DC: Center for Law and Social Policy.

Salomon, A., Bassuk, S., & Brooks, M. (1996). Patterns of welfare use among poor and homeless women. *American Journal of Orthopsychiatry, 66,* 510-525.

Social Security Act of 1975, Title IVA (1975).

Social Security Act of 1988, Title IXX (1988).

U.S. Bureau of the Census. (1995). *Child support for custodial mothers and fathers: 1991* (Current Population Reports, Series P60-187). Washington, DC: Government Printing Office.

U.S. Office of Child Support Enforcement. (1997). *Child support enforcement: 20th annual report to Congress.* Washington, DC: National Reference Center.

6

Domestic Violence Victims and Welfare Services

A Practitioner's View

Diane M. Stuart

The cycle of abuse, a pattern of reoccurring behaviors, is all too familiar to most victims of domestic violence. Confusion, insecurity, and lack of control dominate their lives. They can feel the tension rise; they are constantly on guard, waiting, wondering when "it"—the abuse—will come. No one asks to be abused. No one likes the abuse. But many abuse victims stay because they perceive that they have to. They believe that their abusers will do what they said they would. Their past violence has proved that. The fear is real. The pain is real. The abuser has beaten the woman[1] in the past, and it *is* getting worse; and he said he would harm the children. Some victims stay in abusive relationships because of fear of the unknown, of fear of change. Where can I go? Who will believe me? I'm embarrassed, ashamed. Some stay because they think their abusers really are right: It *is* the women's fault. They *are* to blame. *If only they could love their abusers enough.* Some are isolated from family, friends, other viewpoints besides his. Some stay because they have little education, no jobs, few skills, no alternatives. Some stay for little bits of all of these perceptions combined. Some stay for the children, and some leave because of the children. Some leave for a myriad of other reasons but then go back. Some return several times. When they finally do leave, they leave because they are able to; someone, something has given them the support they need. They have found that there *are* options, resources, choices that can help them be successful in leaving.

This chapter explores some of those options and difficulties within the welfare system, the complexities of those options, and the confidentiality issues that arise for domestic violence victims. It examines the circumstances of women who have had to use welfare services to become independent of their abusers, what the barriers have been for them, and how they have responded to possible revictimizations by the welfare system or other systems, such as the criminal justice system. Reference is made to abusive behaviors, some illustrated on the Power and Control Wheel (Pence & Paymar, 1993), as well as prevention and intervention strategies. Response to the outlined domestic violence complexities is formulated as specific recommendations to state and community agencies, based on my experience as a domestic violence shelter executive director, a state domestic violence specialist, and state coordinator for the Governor's Cabinet Council on Domestic Violence.

Three assumptions drive the discussion. First, *domestic violence is a crime*. Most states' criminal code definition of domestic violence includes specific crimes, such as assault, aggravated assault, criminal homicide, mayhem, harassment, telephone harassment, kidnaping, aggravated kidnaping, stalking, unlawful detention, sexual offenses, and violation of a protective order or ex parte protective order.[2] Second, *victims are not to blame*. Accountability for a domestic violence offense lies with the perpetrator, and not the victim. Third, *domestic violence is preventable* by providing education to agencies, organizations, and individuals who may come in contact with victims of domestic violence, as well as through general societal awareness.

In addition, those working with victims of domestic violence have identified some basic principles as important: First, violence between intimate partners can happen to anyone across any or all socioeconomic statuses. Although poverty and violence are strongly associated (Stark & Flitcraft, 1988), it is not a problem just of the poor and uneducated. A victim of domestic violence who is used to a higher income may also find herself in a position of need for welfare assistance because her abuser has taken all her assets. Second, violence is likely to escalate in severity and frequency over time. Third, power or control or both are often at the center of abusive/violent behaviors. And fourth, patterns of abusive behaviors, though predictable, are often minimized or denied by both the perpetrator and the victim.

Patterns of Abuse

Isolation

Isolation may be physical and social. In Utah, one shelter in the center of the state provides services to five counties with a total population of approximately 55,000 people and that cover more than 20,000 square miles. Workers travel more than 17,000 miles annually to provide services to domestic violence victims (Whitlock, 1996). They need to go where the victim is because the victim may not have transportation, or may fear that her abuser will find her if she leaves, or just does not know where to turn for help. Additionally, many communities in that area are small, rural towns where everyone knows everyone else. With a cultural ethic of individual family responsibility, victims are embarrassed, even ashamed, to ask for assistance, especially if the "family secret" is that she now needs financial and material help because he has beaten her and is in jail. Beyond physical and social isolation, isolation can also be defined in terms of lack of knowledge of resources, options, and help. If a victim is taught by her perpetrator that he is always the one to provide for her needs, the only one who *can* provide for her needs, she may not conceive that other assistance is available to help her obtain independence.

⟐ Case #1

> Sally (all names are fictitious, and accounts are composites of actual events to protect the confidentiality of the individuals involved) was married to Sam for 26 years. They had four children. Sally's name was not on the house, car, or anything else of value that the family had. She had a driver's license, but her name was not on the checking account. Whenever she thought she needed to go to the store to buy groceries or

supplies for the house, she went to Sam with her list for his approval. He would check the list, and if he did not approve of an item, he would hit her in the arm to let her know that he was upset. Then he would give her the amount of money needed to buy the approved groceries. On returning from the store, Sally would present the groceries to Sam, again for approval. And again, if he disapproved of an item, its size, cost, or brand, he would hit her in the arm. Not only that, if Sally had deviated from the prescribed route from their home to the store, another hit. Sam worked hard, he said. Money was hard to come by, and they needed to use it properly for the "good" of the whole family. One day, her son discovered her bruises and insisted that she get help. She did not recognize that she was abused or that there could be another way to live. With the assistance provided from shelter caseworkers, Sally began by applying for food stamps and cash assistance and finding someone to help her budget what money she did have. Over time, she attended university classes and began working to- ward a degree in social work. 🗟

Intimidation

For some women, it may not take long to realize when domestic violence is part of their lives. The violence may come as a shock; nothing like this has ever happened before. No woman expects her man's violence. He wasn't like this before she married him. She didn't see it coming. For Rose, the beating occurred on her honeymoon night.

🗟   Case #2

Rose begged her parents to let her marry Tom, but they did not support her wishes because they did not like him. She waited to marry because it was important to her that her parents approve. Finally, they consented and gave her a beau- tiful wedding. Three days after beating her on their honeymoon night, he returned to the hotel room. He was so sorry; he promised he would never do that again. He didn't. He didn't have to. She knew what he was capable of and for 5 years submitted to his control, intimidated by his every move.

Finally, with the help of her family, she left, turning to state
welfare for support for herself and her small child. ⮐

A victim may perceive that the intimidation extends beyond the
perpetrator's influence, paralyzing her from action. In some cases, a
child may take on the role of the parent when the mother has been
repeatedly traumatized. I have often seen an older child make the
numerous telephone calls for housing, self-sufficiency, and other
assistance programs. Letting a child take over is all Mom can do
because she cannot stop from crying, shaking, and consistently checking to see whether he has found her. She is often paralyzed by the
thought of reaching out on her own.

⮐ Case #3

Shelly, a 9-year-old girl, was constantly asking to come into
the office in a rural shelter for abused women to use the
telephone. After requesting the telephone book, she would sit
and call number after number, setting up appointments for her
mother. She called the Office of Family Support to change their
address for welfare assistance (they needed to go in for an
interview), job service (another interview, of course), the dis-
trict court for the protective order, and the Child and Family
Support Center to care for the younger children while she and
her mother went to all the appointments. During the day, a
call came into my office, demanding to know whether Shelly
and her mother were, in fact, staying at the shelter. The
supervisor of the Office of Family Support was on the line and
wanted me to break confidentiality by letting her know
whether they were indeed residents. I, of course, could not do
that without Shelly's mother's permission. As I put the form
on the desk for a consent signature, Shelly started to sign but
hesitated and then instructed her mother to sign. ⮐

In some cases, the abuser may hold a position of power in the
community, intimidating anyone who may associate with the victim
and, thus, severely limiting assistance to her.

🗐 Case #4

> *Margarita was married to a lawyer who was very prominent in her community. He was popular with his colleagues and was chair of an influential organization of lawyers. When she decided that she wanted a divorce, no one in her community would "take her husband on," as they put it. No one would assist her in any way. He told her to leave and take nothing with her. Through a legal document a friend of his drew up, Margarita's husband made sure she did not have access to his financial or material resources. Eventually, she was forced to leave with a divorce decree that gave him everything and to start again in another city with nothing.* 🗐

Economic Abuse

Margarita's story is also a good illustration of how a perpetrator can impose economic abuse on a victim. Seeking welfare is not restricted to those who have come from poverty backgrounds. Many, like Margarita, who have had a middle-class lifestyle and who are educated may find themselves, through the violent behavior of their partners, in situations with no other alternative but to seek state assistance.

For those who live in depressed areas or areas that have restricted opportunities for work, finding the support and assistance to get into the workforce is extremely difficult. Moab, Utah, for instance, is primarily a tourist town, with few employment opportunities that lead to higher-paying jobs. The workforce is defined by low-paying jobs such a motel maid or waitress, with little or no opportunity for responsibility or income advancement. Coupling the low pay with high rent, victims have few options for financial survival without their perpetrators. Many other communities are also struggling with how to help victims leave abusers when good jobs are scarce and welfare assistance is so limited and complicated with restrictions.

Economic abuse may also appear in other ways, including child care complications (e.g., no licensed provider for children over age 8 or 9) and the sometimes misleading wording on assistance contracts that clients must fill out and sign.

🗐 Case #5

After her abusive husband was arrested, Shondra, assisted by the shelter caseworker, applied for any assistance she could for herself and her four boys. She filled out her paperwork by honestly answering the questions asked. She was asked how much her rent was, and she answered $478. She was not asked what portion of that amount she paid and what portion housing assistance paid. Six months later, when she had her review, she was asked for the same information, but this time the question was worded differently. This time, it specifically asked who paid what portion. Again, she answered honestly and provided the details asked for. After her paperwork was reviewed, she was informed that she had to return to the state the unauthorized money she received because her rent was supplemented by housing assistance. 🗐

Emotional Abuse

"Mind games" are often played by a perpetrator of domestic violence. He does all he can to make the woman feel and think as though her feelings, her knowledge of the event, is mistaken.

🗐 Case #6

Beth and Bill were fighting in the kitchen one morning before work when Bill leaned over and shoved Beth into the kitchen cabinet corner. He then walked out of the room and into the bedroom to get ready. Beth returned to her dishes, noticing after a short period of time that her head began to throb. She went out of the kitchen through the bedroom, where Bill was, and headed to the bathroom to get some aspirin. She was rubbing her head as she walked. Bill stopped her and asked what was the matter. She told him that she must have hit her head when Bill shoved her and that it now hurt. Bill began screaming what a baby she was, that he never even touched her, and that it was all "in her mind." He said that she wanted to be hurt and so she thought she was. Nothing could be further from the truth, he said. Beth began to wonder if it was her imagination. She had not felt good that morning. Maybe she really didn't want to go to work. 🔊

Often, an abuser will fight the night before or engage in a verbal or psychological attack just as the woman is going out the door for work. He may tell her that she is stupid (can't you remember anything?), doesn't really look nice (you're not really going to wear *that*, are you?), or otherwise tear down her ability to concentrate at work. He may call her several times during the day (to talk about nothing) and remind her that she never considers his day or his problems.

Coercion

Coercion is a manipulative tool used by a perpetrator of domestic violence when he knows that the victim is devoted to him. For example, a victim often thinks that she is the only one who can help her abuser. She is, after all, the one who loves him the most and the one who knows him better than anyone else. She cannot tell anyone what is really happening or she will lose her ability to help him. He knows that she will do anything for him, and with that knowledge he forces her to lie for him, cover up for him, even steal for him. He may convince her that he will leave, for example, if she does not write just one bad check or if she does not steal items from work. She knows it is wrong, but she is convinced that he will leave if she doesn't do as he asks, and she is the only one who can help him change.

🔊 **Case #7**

Suzanne was referred to the shelter by the judge. She had been arrested for forging checks and was in jail. We went to see her and talked about how she got there. Over the course of several visits, we learned that she was in an abusive relationship. She stayed because she loved him so much. She knew that he had problems, but she thought that, over time, her influence would straighten him out. But it was Suzanne who was in jail. To protect him from a bad debt, she had written the check and had got caught. She was now out of work, had a felony record, and knew that she would have a difficult time getting another job. 🔊

This becomes an important issue for states that have taken the option to *not* serve convicted felons through their Temporary Assistance for Needy Families (TANF) program or their Food Stamp Program. Other states, such as Utah, have decided that they will provide financial assistance to those convicted of felonies.

Obstacles

Obstacles impeding individuals seeking welfare assistance may be numerous and complex without the added complication of domestic violence. Often, deterrents to obtaining assistance include a lack of knowledge of which agency has what resource; an urgent need for transportation, especially in remote, rural areas; and the stigma attached to someone who may be viewed as lazy, helpless, and/or ignorant. Welfare experiences for domestic violence victims are compounded by their abuse, traumatization, and exploitation.

Access to Services

A main concern for many domestic violence victims is access to welfare services. The questions of finding effective assistance and meeting all the necessary requirements, or the perceived shame associated with needing help, are complicated by the dynamics associated with domestic violence.

In a series of focus groups with victims of domestic violence held recently in Utah (Jones & Associates, 1996), victims were asked, "Can victims get help?" The revealing answers included "Yes, if you look hard enough," "Options are available, but you have to be PERSISTENT," and "It took a nervous breakdown to get help." These are troubling responses, considering the state of mind of many victims of domestic violence. Fear does not often allow a victim to look hard enough, be persistent, or even understand that she might be experiencing psychological trauma. Consider Isabelle:

🗐 Case #8

Isabelle came to the shelter, wanting to do all she could to end the violence in her life. She was ready to leave her husband

and, with help, had applied for food stamps and AFDC. Isabelle had always been told that she was to stay at home and care for the children. She didn't know any places to get help; she had never been allowed to ask for any assistance. Her husband had told her that he would take care of her. While in the shelter, she submitted applications for several jobs, but with her lack of experience, she was turned down for all of them. Isabelle spent hours on the telephone, trying to get work; she even had a friend ask around for her. While Isabelle was at the shelter, her abuser came to the back gate and pointed a gun at her children, who came into the shelter, screaming. He fled before law enforcement arrived, and they were never able to gather enough evidence to prove that he was there. Isabelle returned to him within the week. ☙

System Abuse

One victim I recently spoke with felt as though she was abused by the system as she attempted to improve her ability to get a good-paying job when she started back to school to earn a 4-year degree in elementary education. She was receiving state assistance at the time, and her caseworker told her that she would not be able to continue in her educational pursuits because she could not finish within the newly established 2-year time frame; she must make do with a 2-year associate's degree. Having completed her associate's degree, she is now finding, however, that she cannot support her three children with an "associate's" income. It just isn't enough money to live on, not to mention paying back any loans that assisted her in her educational pursuit. She is as trapped as she ever was, often feeling that the control has been transferred from the perpetrator to the state. Restricted time frames such as this are the result of the new welfare reform rules implemented in many states. Other states have adopted similar rules, including for some a ban on a college education completely.

The relationship between an abused mother and her child is a difficult situation for welfare workers to understand. Many workers are young, do not have children of their own, and often do not have any experience of what it is like for children who have lived in an abusive home. Some, often without adequate training, very quickly take the parental authority from the mother and give it to the child.

🗿 Case #9

Rebekah's husband often beat her in front of their four boys, degrading her and telling the boys that their mother deserved this treatment. Their 13-year-old son became, over time, just as abusive to his mother as his father was. Additionally, as is often the pattern with boys with abusive fathers, the oldest son also hit, shoved, shouted at, and swore at his three younger brothers, using expletives that would cause most to be alarmed. When he and his mother visited with the state assistance welfare worker, this young man told the worker that his mother had slapped his face (omitting that she was responding to his cursing). Without any hesitation, this worker turned to the young man and told him that his mother is not allowed to do that in this state and that she can be turned in for child abuse if she does. 🗿

Confidentiality

Those who work in welfare services are, for the most part, knowledgeable about confidentiality procedures and careful about appropriate applications. A lack of understanding of the possible lethality issues when working with a victim of domestic violence, however, may put that victim in extreme danger. Consider the following account:

🗿 Case #10

Hiding from an extremely violent partner, Mai began to rebuild her life. She entered a transitional housing program and began working. The purpose of the program is to help women who have been abused gain the skills they need to avoid future instances of homelessness through financial employment and residential stability. When Mai applied for AFDC, she was told that she needed to sign a child support waiver. The caseworker explained good cause policy, but Mai was under a tremendous amount of stress at the time and did not give it much thought. Recently, she was notified by the Office of Recovery Services that her ex-husband's wages were going to be garnished for payment of back child support for their daughter. Because of the process of being contacted by the authorities in the state where she lives, her ex-husband now knows what state she lives in. He had previously told Mai that he would kill her and their child rather than pay child support. During their marriage, he had tried to shoot her and had thrown her down a flight of stairs. Today, Mai fears for her life, as she believes that he will find her and carry out his threats. When she informed the child support office of her situation and the danger it had created, the staff reacted in an unconcerned manner and informed her that she might have to relocate or stay in a safe house. 🔊

When victims in the focus groups mentioned earlier were asked about welfare services, their answers included "I'm tired of people who know everything about me," "I need help NOW—it takes 5 days to get food stamps—too much lag time," and "We need one-stop-shopping, one sheet to fill out." Victims may be pushed across several systems (criminal justice, health care, social service) sometimes extremely quickly and often without help or experience on which to draw. Then, when a victim meets with a worker for public assistance and experience has shown her that she may have to talk about her situation "one more time," she may be resigned to that stressful task, but a worker may not be sensitive to the signs of abuse.

🔊   Case #11

Terri met with her caseworker and began the process of obtaining help through the state welfare system. Although she was currently in a violent marriage and had often been beaten by her husband, she never disclosed this to her worker. It seemed to be none of the worker's business. Then one day, Terri had to meet with the caseworker after a terrible fight. Her ribs were extremely sore, and she had a black eye. She came to the appointment early, and as she told the receptionist that she was there, she saw her caseworker through the window. The caseworker looked straight at her and then turned away. The receptionist asked Terri to sit in the waiting room, which was full of other welfare clients. The waiting room was a fairly large, open area and was also used for access to other agencies in the building. Terri sat waiting for 15 minutes amid the stares and seemingly obvious unasked questions of the other clients. When Terri finally went in to see the caseworker, nothing was said about her eye. Their appointment proceeded as usual. ✍

Recommendations for Implementation of Welfare Reform

Specific recommendations for welfare case managers cover several areas of concern, including assessment, privacy or confidentiality, evidence, universal education, and training.

Assessment

- Provide information about domestic violence and available resources, such as counseling, shelters, health care, and legal services, each time applicants and recipients interact with welfare workers. This allows the applicant or recipient ongoing opportunities to disclose any abuse when she is ready and feels safe to do so.

  Provide information through multiple and creative means, such as brochures, posters, palm cards, stickers, and waiting room videos.
- Require only as much information from the applicant or recipient as necessary to refer to services and determine eligibility for waivers or exemptions.
- Provide flexible times to meet with applicants or recipients (e.g., before 8 a.m., after 5 p.m.), allowing them some control in selecting an appropriate time.
- Address risk factors when negotiating plans.

Privacy

- Discuss with the applicant or recipient the reasons for, and the consequences of, disclosing any information about the applicant/recipient.
- Obtain written permission to disclose information about the applicant or recipient.
- Disclose only the amount of information (limited information) necessary to accomplish the reason for contacting an agency, organization, or person about an applicant or recipient.
- In most cases, an individual affidavit that abuse has occurred should meet the burden of proof.

- Do not contact any person believed to be the perpetrator for the purpose of corroborating evidence.
- Do not disclose any information that may endanger the recipient.

Training

- Training for welfare workers should address domestic violence issues, including

    Dynamics, definitions, and general information about available legal remedies and resources

    Screening issues, with an emphasis on providing information to all clients (universal notification)

    Casework issues, including ways an abusive partner may sabotage a victim's ability to work

    The state's procedures for exemptions or extensions, and referral issues, including how to make an effective referral
- Cross-training must be provided among agencies, such as domestic violence shelters and victim assistance programs. Domestic violence shelters and victim assistance programs need to learn about welfare reform, and welfare workers need to learn about the expertise in domestic violence programs.

Additionally, corporate collaboration is essential. As job placement agencies are eager to learn their role and their responsibility, they need to extend their resources to meet the needs of all members of the community, including, of course, those who have been victimized by others. Businesses, governmental agencies, and schools must react in a creative, effective manner. Many workplaces have requested education programs, such as the Utah Attorney General's *Safe at Home* program (Graham, 1996), or have put together their own programs with the assistance of the Family Violence Prevention Fund.[3] These programs are intended to reach victims, offenders, or their friends, neighbors, and loved ones at their places of business. The 1-hour presentation of the *Safe at Home* program includes a short video presentation dramatizing the problems and calling to action those who participate in the program. The video is supplemented by live presentations from experts who explain the dynamics of domestic violence, recommend solutions to those involved in violent relationships, and provide local resources, followed by a question-and-answer period. More than 50,000 employees have been made aware of the dynamics of domestic violence (Graham, 1998), and many have made changes in their lives as a result of similar programs.

Finally, it is recommended that states commit the resources necessary for local domestic violence programs and for welfare service programs to provide victims with the help they need to be safe and economically secure. Referral services must exist, be accessible, and respond in culturally sensitive ways. All departments, human or social services *and* welfare services, need to do all they can to reduce the risk to victims of domestic violence and to document programs that work.

Notes

1. For ease of narrative, a victim of domestic violence will be referred to as a female and the perpetrator as a male. I do, of course, acknowledge that the batterer may be a woman and the victim may be a male.

2. A *protective order* is an order issued by the court, designed to give victims of domestic violence protection by preventing the abuser from having contact with, threatening, or entering onto the property of the victim. An ex parte protective order can be issued the day the victim asks for it, without the abuser being present. Once the abuser is given a copy of the order, it is effective until a court hearing is held, where the abuser is invited to be present. After a court hearing, the court can issue a protective order that is effective for a specific time or until further order of the court. Conditions of protective orders within each state will vary according to state statute.

3. Family Violence Prevention Fund, 383 Rhode Island Street, Suite 304, San Francisco, CA 94103.

References

Graham, J. (1996). *Safe at home: Every Utahn has a right to be* [Videotape]. Available from Office of the Attorney General, Salt Lake City, UT.

Graham, J. (1998). *Safe at home impact* [Brochure]. Available from Office of the Attorney General, Salt Lake City, UT.

Jones, D., & Associates, Inc. (1996). *Qualitative research analysis.* Conducted on behalf of the Governor's Commission for Women and Families, Violence Against Women Survey Committee, Salt Lake City, UT.

Pence, E., & Paymar, M. (1993). *Education groups for men who batter: The Duluth model.* New York: Springer.

Stark, E., & Flitcraft, A. (1988). Violence among intimates: An epidemiological review. In V. Van Hasselt, R. Morrison, A. Bellack, & M. Hersen (Eds.), *Handbook of family violence* (pp. 293-297). New York: Plenum.

Whitlock, L. (1996). *New Horizons Crisis Center: 1995 statistics.* Richfield, UT: New Horizons Crisis Center.

7

Voices of the Women

Survivors of Domestic Violence and Welfare

Annie Boone
Ginger Erickson
Melissa Arch-Walton

The first discussion was written by Annie Boone.

I guess that every time I share my life experience with anyone, it becomes just a little easier to deal with. I remember that, the first time I had shared my story, I broke down in tears and became really choked up. I (of course) was crying so hard that I could not get the words out. It was so embarrassing. Reality hit quickly; I still felt anger, betrayal, resentment, and humiliation. How could I share the "big secret" that I had held on to for 14 years?

I grew up in a very religious family. I was raised with some very strong morals and values that I was expected to live up to. From a very young age, I was taught that the man of the house was the breadwinner and that his word was law even if you disagreed. My role was to be a good wife, mother, and cook. I was not to go to work. I was just to make sure there was a loving environment for my husband and children. Most of all, I learned that marriage was a commitment and that adultery was an absolute "NO." I should have no other needs, wants, or desires. I should be fulfilled if I had accomplished this task. Most important, I would be pleasing God.

I also learned that my father had a very bad temper; I would be better off if I did not disagree with him. His word was law, and I had better not disobey it. I always thought that he went overboard with punishment and abuse. As children, we all grew to expect his wrath. Of course, now I look back and realize that my father did not know the first thing about parenting. He had lost both of his parents by the age of 15. I did not like my dad much growing up, but I was taught either to have respect for him or else.

My parents were very strict. My mother was always sick, and I felt as though all the family responsibility was dropped off on me because I was the oldest. I took care of my brother and sister as though they were my own children. I also went to school and worked. My parents also insisted that I pay rent to live with them even at the age of 14. There was no such thing as free time. I needed my own space and some freedom. I had grown way beyond my years. I also thought that, because I had so much responsibility, I should be able to have just a few privileges.

I started dating a guy I met from one of the jobs I had held during the summer months. I sneaked around a lot just to see him. I started running away from home. I would not come home at curfew. I just wanted to have some fun. My parents got very angry and kicked me out at the age of 15. I came home one day to find that the personal belongings they would allow me to have were packed and outside on the porch. My father told me that I was not welcome in their home anymore because I could not follow the rules.

My girlfriend's parents took me in, and I still worked and went to school. After living away from home for a while, I went back for a visit to see how things were going. My father and I had a discussion about my boyfriend, and I told my father that we were thinking about moving in together and sharing expenses. He became really angry and told me that if I chose to do that he would call the police and tell them that I had run away. He told me that the best option for all of us was just for me to marry my boyfriend. I did not want to come back home. For once, I was having fun and did not have to fear my father.

My boyfriend and I had discussed marriage, but we were thinking later on in life. I discussed this problem with my boyfriend, and we decided that it was time to take away the control my father had over my life and my happiness. We decided, ready or not, that we would just get married.

We got married on May 1, 1978. I walked down the aisle so full of pride. I found it funny that everyone was gossiping about how I must be pregnant to get married so young. I found it amusing that they had just assumed the worst. I don't think the people gossiping really wanted to hear the truth about anything. I was determined to show them it was not true. I was going to make this marriage work no matter what.

Little did I know that I was leaving one abusive relationship for another. It was not long before I saw another side of my husband that I had not seen before we got married. He was very controlling. He did not like my friends around. He had pretty much made sure they felt uncomfortable coming over to see me. If I had money, he took it. I kept telling myself that he would change in time. I tried very hard to be patient and understanding. I would never tell anyone that happily married me was being abused. I also did not realize that having children would be used as a tool or an excuse for him to take off for parts unknown (sometimes a few days at a time). He would take the bill money and spend it on alcohol and drugs. I was always left wondering how I was going to pay the bills. He became increasingly abusive. I was awakened at odd hours of the night and told to cook dinner and fulfill his sexual desires. I learned that it was easier to comply than suffer the consequences for not complying.

By the age of 20, I was pregnant with our third child. My husband came home one day and told me about a lady who was having a very hard time with two boys and needed a place to stay. I felt sorry for her and decided to let her stay at our house. I had no idea what a mistake that would be. I soon realized that my husband and my new roommate would disappear for hours at a time, leaving me at home to baby-sit all of the children. I suspected things were not right and tried to believe that this was not happening. My marriage was not working. The things I had been taught kept running through my mind: It is not okay to have an adulterous relationship. I finally got the courage to confront my husband about the affair. He finally admitted to the affair and told me that he was going to tell me but that he had wanted to wait until after Christmas (which was only 2 weeks away)!

I was devastated. I could not believe that he would actually have the nerve to bring his lover into our home. Then the worst news—she might be pregnant with his child. After days of not sleeping, I decided it was over. I would leave and get on with my life. I could finally rest. I lay down but soon realized that my husband was home. I was awakened by my husband, and I pretended that I did not hear him. He got so angry that he threw a cold pitcher of water on me. I chose to lie there and not respond to him. He went and got another pitcher of water and threw it on me. By the third time, with no response, he grabbed me by my shirt and pants and threw me to the floor. I jumped up, worried about the child I was pregnant with, and started asking him, "How could you do this to me?" I was crying and desperately needed to understand. He told me that he wanted me to watch my roommate's children so that the two of them could go have a drink at the bar. I told him no, I would not watch her children so that the two of them could go out. My roommate walked into the room and said, "Why don't you just grow up?" I lost my temper and called my roommate a name that my husband did not like. He punched me in the face and then grabbed me by the throat. I was gasping for air. Blood started flowing from my mouth. My oldest son was crying and pleading with his father not to hit his mommy anymore. That broke my heart. I was concerned about the baby I was carrying and the shirt I had borrowed from the neighbor. I finally felt defeated and watched her children. I could not stand to see my children hurting. I was so ashamed. I finally got the courage to call my father. Between spells of tears, I asked for my family's help. I needed out, I needed to feel safe. After I talked with my father, my roommate called and asked me whether I thought my husband would ever do that to her. I told her, "I hope for your sake he never does," but in my heart I knew he would.

By the next morning, my father had arranged for five trucks to help me move. I was determined this time never to go back to my husband. He could abuse me, but by God, he was not going to get his cake and eat it too. Three weeks after I moved out of our home, my husband came knocking at my parents' house. He told me that he wanted me back and that he was sorry. I told him that I was not going to go back to him ever. I now had to deal with his harassment. He came to my parents' home several times drunk and making threats. He stalked me. He got into a fight with one of my friends in front of our children. I was beginning to wonder whether I could ever break free from him. My parents were worried for my safety and theirs. They finally told me that I would have to find another place to live because they could not afford to take care of me and my family. They were also afraid that my husband would try to do something stupid.

I was beginning to feel very defeated—no money and no place to go. I was just trying to provide emotional stability for my family. I was definitely a basket case. I was emotionally traumatized. I finally had the nerve to ask for assistance. My family needed a safe place to call home. After a lot of paperwork and investigation to make sure that I was not living with my husband, I finally received assistance. Now I could find us a place of our own.

I am very concerned about all of these policy changes in the welfare system. I think it is detrimental to women trying to escape domestic violence. I don't like the idea that women may have to choose between staying with their abusers to financially survive or becoming homeless, hungry, and living in very desperate situations.

In Utah, we have a 3-year lifetime limit on public assistance, whereas the federal guideline is 5 years. Without assistance, I may not have been able to escape my abuser. I want other women in the same situation to be able to flee if necessary. If they feel trapped and don't have any choice, they may stay with abusers who may kill them. I don't know many women who admit they are being abused by loved ones. It is a far greater risk to admit to some caseworker that you are or have been abused. I think that if society really knew the options for women in these situations, people would rather help them make a safe easy escape. There are too many stereotypes about the welfare system and the women and children on it. The saddest part about it is that society really believes that women feel comfortable in the system and that they are just lazy and have no desire to get jobs.

I can't begin to tell you the obstacles that women face once they finally get the courage to leave. I was terrified of the world. I had very little trust for anyone. Going to the store by myself was an accomplishment. I had extreme headaches from being hit in the face and head area so many times. They would be so intense that I would close myself in a dark room and lie there motionless for hours at a time. I went to the emergency room at one point, and the doctor had given me so much pain medicine that he was astounded I was still awake and in intense pain. They made me stay the night. No matter how many drugs they gave me, the headache was not going away.

My two boys who had witnessed the abuse were traumatized. One son acted out and was angry and destroyed toys, property, or whatever he could get his hands on, including his own mother. His behavior was overwhelming. I lost several jobs because the school or day care or a baby-sitter did not want to deal with his behavior. He now is serving time in an adult jail, in an adult world, all at the age of 16, for actions he saw often as a child. Their father continued to tell his children that if it were not for their mother, we would still be a family. It is all your mother's fault. Their father also told them that I deserved to be abused because I was a bitch.

I have to say that if it were not for the welfare system, I probably would not be here today to share my story of why women and children exist on the welfare system. Their lives depend on it.

My ex-husband has a track record of abusing women. He spent this last October in jail for assault of his newest victim. This last summer, my oldest son thought it might be nice to visit his father, whom he had not seen in 11 years. His father kicked my son out on his 17th birthday after assaulting him for trying to protect his father's girlfriend from being abused. My son was only there for 2 weeks. I think he has a new awareness of what his father is capable of.

My ex-husband tells me that I will never see a dime of child support because I refused to take him back. He owes me and the state of Utah $61,000. I think that the whole focus in the welfare system needs to look at the bigger picture. Women do not have these children alone. Where are the fathers? We always blame the women. I did not ask to be born with reproductive organs so that I could be blamed for what my body was intended to do. I don't think it is fair or right for others to judge me or to place blame.

I hope that people who read this have changed their minds about the myths or assumptions they may have had about women on welfare. I am no longer on the welfare system, but it was an awful struggle to get off. Without the support, I don't think I would have made it.

I work for Justice, Economic Dignity, and Independence for Women (JEDI Women) as their lead organizer. I have gained so much knowledge and strength from this organization. Most important, I have learned that many women have experienced some form of violence in their lifetimes and that I am not alone. There is power in numbers. Women must stand together and speak out. If you keep the "big secret," it allows the abuser to keep on abusing over and over again. Women need to take back their power. More important, we as parents need to make sure we teach our daughters that they must be educated and be independent. They must be told that their greatest role in life is to love themselves.

T he second discussion was written by Ginger Erickson.

My welfare experience involves domestic violence and the laws that allowed my husband to qualify and keep me on public assistance.

In 1993, I married my second husband. During our short-term marriage, he beat me twice. (He was subsequently convicted of two counts of assault.) During the second beating, I was pregnant and threatening to miscarry. After the beating was over, I vowed that my child would not be raised by a violent man. He never apologized, but told me only that I deserved it, that he would do it again, and that he learned from the first time—not to leave any marks. He told me that he wished I would miscarry because it would make our divorce less complicated. I knew that I had to leave him. I was afraid that I would lose my baby if he beat me again.

I didn't know how I was going to leave him. I had a job, but I didn't have a car, I didn't have any money saved, and I didn't have a place to live. Leaving your husband is not like planning a vacation: You have to leave, whether you are ready or not. I left my ex-husband the next time he became explosively angry with me. I was not ready.

Becoming a mother is what kept body and soul together. Because of my great desire to be at home to raise my child, I found an at-home night job. I kept my full-time day job and trained with this company part-time at night to meet my financial goals.

Between the stress of my divorce and working too many hours, I frequented Labor and Delivery for fetal monitoring. My obstetrician ordered me to reduce my hours of work. I left my full-time job. With my decreased income, I applied for Aid to Families With Dependent Children (AFDC) and food stamps. I was denied the assistance.

My son, Danny, was born May 27, 1994. Because of continued lost wages, I reapplied for welfare and food stamp assistance. I qualified for these programs June 1st.

Shortly after delivery, my son needed oxygen; he was put under an oxygen tent, given antibiotics, and had X rays taken. After release, he needed phototherapy, developed infections and fevers, had a spinal tap, and at 3 months had tubes placed in his ears. By 5 months, Danny was diagnosed with immune mediated neutropenia—a blood disorder. This condition made it imperative that he be kept away from controllable sick exposures (specifically, group day care environments).

I took on an additional at-home job to help meet my financial needs. I was not yet recuperated, I had had a difficult delivery, and I was exhausted. I averaged 4 hours of interrupted sleep each night.

Exhaustion brought on because of the lack of sleep caused me to leave my employment. I hoped soon to return to work for these companies. After leaving these jobs, I received a full AFDC allotment. At this point, I started feeling the pressures of the state's now self-sufficiency program. I was panic stricken at the thought that a time table might be instituted in my county and that I could lose the much-needed assistance.

I applied to the JTPA (Job Training Partnership Act) program. By the time school started, my son's quarantine was lifted. I completed two quarters of school with straight A's by August 1995. My employment interviews never yielded an offer.

Between October 1995 and February 1996, my son started having regular infections and fevers again. He was taken to the emergency room because he suffered a seizure; there he was given an EEG (electroencephalogram) and an audiology test, and a second set of tubes was inserted. I accepted a strictly commission sales job so that I could have the flexibility to care for my son.

Because of a significant number of infections, Danny's immune system was tested. With the assurance that he could fight off whatever he might catch at a day care center, I resumed interviewing for a competitive salary job. Again, I was never offered a position. By good fortune, I found an ideal day care center where I could immediately place my son. Even better, I have been working since March 18, 1996, for this center where my son is now enrolled. I have been off AFDC since April 1, 1996.

I would have been off AFDC in 1994 had the state laws allowed the Office of Recovery Services (Child Support Enforcement) to compute my ex-husband's full income. Shortly after I filed for divorce, he changed careers. For the past 3 years, he has earned $7,000 annually. In the 3 years prior to our marriage, he earned more than $30,000 a year. He now works an average of only 10 days each month.

Had the state laws not allowed my ex-husband—who is healthy and free from illness and disability—to maintain paper poverty, the original child support calculation would have disqualified me from receiving AFDC assistance. Because the court ruled that he was within his right to change his career, I am now shorted additional child support.

What more could I have done to circumvent the need for public assistance? I have done all I could to help myself and my son. What would I have done if these assistance programs were not available to me?

A horrid stigma is attached to being a welfare recipient. We are there because we need to be. We are there because we need financial help raising the children whom our men have abandoned. Our stories differ, but the needs are the same.

I do not feel sorry for myself. Despite my son's health concerns, he is a very fit, thriving child. Through all the stresses and hard times I face, I pay every price so that my son will never have to. This is his childhood. I want only to serve my son well.

A national children's advocacy organization aptly states: It takes time, patience, love, understanding, and money to raise a child.

It is unfortunate that, along with motherhood, I found poverty, a poverty my ex-husband and state laws allowed. Money alone does not raise a happy child, but it does take money.

Danny is my heartbeat. I love him endlessly.

The third discussion was written by Melissa Arch-Walton.

Domestic violence is an insidious demon. It, like the abuser himself, never stands right up and announces itself. Instead, you wake up one day, lying on your back in bed, with sore ribs, a headache, and a black eye, and realize that you are being abused. You wonder: How did it come to this? How did love turn into something that hurts like hell and scares me to death?

My husband never announced that, at the 3-month mark in our relationship, he would begin to punctuate his statements with his hands. He worked up to that casually and, I believe, without any idea himself that one day he would try to beat me and my children half to death. Domestic violence for me began with small comments from him about how he believed that I could dress, act, sit, walk, or respond in more appropriate ways.

This "constructive criticism" turned into berating and mentally and emotionally abusive diatribes about my weight and my gregarious personality. He didn't like the way I said hello to strangers in stores or gas stations, and he didn't like the way I "looked" at other guys. My style of dress was criticized and corrected until he was sure there was not too much flesh showing when I went out of the house. I even remember a particularly nasty fight that commenced when he became angered because I had shown up at his job with his lunch but without makeup. "Don't you ever come to my job looking like that again, or you'll be sorry you left the house," he screamed.

This vicious cycle fed itself so that, for every fault of mine that he pointed out, I attempted to correct whatever it was I had been doing wrong. This was done on my part without the realization that I could do nothing that would actually satisfy him. He simply pointed out somewhere else that I had been deficient, and then he would berate me into believing that I was stupid, fat, worthless, and lazy. It is not difficult to understand how it is possible to find that, after 3 months of being reminded of your every fault, the first time you are hit you believe that you deserve it; after all, you are lazy and stupid, aren't you?

During my first pregnancy, an argument ensued on the way back from dinner at my sister-in-law's house that culminated in my being thrown out of the car on a deserted strip of highway. I stood there waiting for my husband to come back and pick me up. When he did return a few minutes later, he yelled at me for looking stupid standing out in the road and demanded that I get back in the car. I simply stared at him, trying to imagine how a man leaves his wife, 6 months pregnant with his first child, standing on the side of the road, crying.

When I did not climb back in the car fast enough, he got out and came around to my side to make me get into the car. This he did by grabbing me by the hair on the back of my head and slamming my head into the side of the car before opening the car door and shoving me inside. I sat on the passenger's side, holding my head and crying hysterically, while he got in on the driver's side of the car and told me to stop making such a scene. "You know," he reminded me, "this would never happen if you would just do what I tell you to do in the first place."

I began by stating that domestic violence is insidious, that it sneaks up on you and you don't realize you are being abused until it is too late and you feel totally enmeshed in a situation that is not of your making. The welfare system can be like that too.

Welfare was my only way out of the ridiculously abusive marriage in which I felt trapped. If it had been unavailable to my children and me, I am sure we would not have survived long enough for me to be writing about this today. I was brought up in a very religious family that believed marriage is sacred and that, regardless of how painful and insane a marriage is, God wants those two people to remain married forever. Without the support of my family when I left the marriage, there was nowhere else to turn except the Department of Social Services.

Imagine my relief when I was placed in a "safe house" approximately 40 miles from my family and friends, where sleep was impossible because of the necessity of staying awake the entire night to keep the roaches off my children while they slept! We were placed in a one-room efficiency apartment, with no counseling, no access to transportation, and no way to communicate with those we had left behind when we fled.

I had never used food stamps in my life, and I was distinctly unprepared for the raw anger that was aimed at me in grocery stores in a town that was foreign to me. There was no way for me to explain to each person who looked at me as if I had stolen the food directly out of their refrigerators that I was living with the fear of discovery by my husband and the abuse that would accompany that revelation. I never grew accustomed to the inhumane treatment by the welfare workers who treated me like a walking infectious disease. Wasn't it their job to help me feed my children and find work and housing? If so, then why were they so mad at me for asking for the assistance I needed?

I remember thinking that I would rather put up with the abuse from my husband than the abuse from the social services system. Nationwide statistics show that women go back to their abusers an average of eight times before they are either killed or leave the men for the last time. I understand why. When presented with the choice of being perceived as just another woman of color on welfare with "illegitimate children" or as a "good" wife, I chose the latter four times before I left my husband for good.

Many people tried to convince me that for my children to have a bad father was better than having no father in the house at all. I believed that for a long time and castigated myself for not being able to hang in there. But, eventually, I realized that my children's lives were in jeopardy as much or more than my own, and I made the choice to live on the less than subsistence standards of welfare until I could do better.

It constantly amazes me that the people making laws in Congress are so out of touch with the realities of being poor in America that they actually believe that the choice to live on welfare is a luxurious choice. That my children and I are buying clothes at the Salvation Army store with the $25 left in my monthly grant for clothing and stretching beans and hot dogs with rice are a testament to the fact that we do not live as well as the members of Congress, whose checks are paid out of the public dole like mine.

Welfare was only a choice for me when the question was a matter of life or death. I chose to live, regardless of how meager that living turned out to be. My decision was no different from that of dozens of other women I have spoken with who have told similar stories of abuse and the rapid descent into poverty that followed their decision to leave abusive situations. It may be politically expedient to turn the middle class against the poor in our society, but it does nothing to address how poverty reduces and subjugates those who live within its confines, it certainly does not address the real question, which is, Why do we accept the profound disparity between the rich and the poor in this country?

PART III

CHILD ABUSE

8

Doing the Triple Combination

Negotiating the Domestic Violence, Child Welfare, and Welfare Systems

Diana May Pearce

When women experience domestic violence, their children may also be abused, physically or sexually or both, at rates estimated to range from 28% to 70% of the children involved (McKay, 1994; studies cited by Peled, 1997). Just *witnessing* domestic violence is defined in some states as abuse, which would bring the proportion close to 100%. Even without experiencing the abuse directly, there is little doubt that children are negatively affected; they often exhibit more social, emotional, and behavioral problems than children from nonviolent homes (Peled, 1997). Many times, these children become of concern to the child welfare system.

Conflicting Perspectives

Because of the involvement of children, when women who encounter domestic violence seek help, they often find themselves caught between systems with quite different priorities, perspectives, and policies. Children are the primary focus of the child welfare system, whereas today's welfare system concentrates on women—specifically, moving mothers into paid employment. To further complicate things, women are also the central focus of the battered women's movement, although with a very different emphasis—that of empowerment. As a result, women find themselves subject to conflicting advice and demands from domestic violence services and child welfare and welfare officials. Indeed, sometimes a mother will find that whereas one agency requires that she enter employment, another will insist that she be at home to protect her children from the abusive parent. Below, I discuss the perspectives of different helping institutions and then examine how they affect women clients.

The Domestic Violence/Battered Women's Movement

The domestic violence, or battered women's movement was largely an outgrowth of the revived women's movement of the 1970s. The movement developed an analysis of domestic violence that held abused women harmless and blamed male violence on a larger culture that condones violence as a way of solving problems, that supports male violence against women, and that supports patriarchy and the economic dependence of women on men. Indeed, worldwide, an effort has been made to make domestic violence a crime, to take it out of the "private" realm of family, and to make women who experience abuse crime victims (Mills, 1996). This perspective continues today with efforts of domestic violence advocates to criminalize marital rape and to secure probable-cause arrest policies and more effective protection orders.

Although the women's movement reframed the question of wife abuse—shifting the blame for violence away from the woman—the services provided by shelters sought to engender in these women a view of themselves, not as victims, but as agents of their own lives, capable of creating new lives for themselves and their families. The more radical feminists have seen battered women's shelters as the cutting edge of the women's movement, the place where women could renounce all the myths surrounding marriage, reject the feminine mystique, and become fully human. Women's shelters are even seen by some radical feminists as the stepping stone for women to create separatist communities. Of course, most women going through the shelters have been much more mainstream, seeing their problems as less systemic than personal, having to do with themselves and their own abusers, and many return again and again to their abusers.

Although the focus is on the mother, many in the battered women's movement have become increasingly aware of the traumatic impact on children of domestic violence and the high incidence of child abuse in families with domestic violence. Indeed, a survey of programs for victims of domestic abuse found that two thirds of homes or programs for battered women also had programs for the children (National Coalition Against Domestic Violence, 1991; cited in Peled, 1997). At the same time, children have been seen consistently as "secondary victims" by the battered women's movement. The dominant model assumes that treating, helping, and empowering the mother would end the abuse and, indirectly, be a "treatment" for the child. Evidence does suggest that removing a child from a domestic violence situation greatly lessens the child's likelihood of being abused by the abusive partner or by the abused mother (Peled, 1997). Programs within battered women's shelters have come to acknowledge this co-occurrence of abuse of children together with their mothers and increasingly have brought various kinds of therapy to deal with it, but they are still in the context of the *mother* being the primary victim. Because resources are often scarce, this has sometimes meant that when choices have to be made, services are funded first for the "primary" victims—the mothers.

The Child Welfare System

In contrast, the perspective of the child welfare system is that the *child* is the primary victim regardless of the circumstances in the family as a whole. Furthermore, it often expects even more of the mother than of the father in the sense that although the father/abuser may lose much or all contact with the children, at the same time he is not held responsible for their welfare.[1] In contrast, the mother is expected to take on increased responsibility for the emotional as well as economic well-being of her children. The child welfare system expects her to be omniscient, nurturing, and a strong and self-activated person. The child welfare system demands that mothers not only know about any abuse by adult males but also prevent or counteract it as well. In other words, women are held responsible for *both* their male partners' behavior *and* the protection of their children.

Although the domestic violence movement sees the victimization of women and children as part of a larger societal characteristic of patriarchy and economic and social inequality of women, the child welfare system does not explicitly acknowledge the unequal position of women in society. By asserting a false equality between women and men, it often ends up blaming the woman for the abuse that happens to her children.

The Welfare System

The above-mentioned two perspectives clash in the welfare system, which itself is ambivalent and often contradictory. On the one hand, the original federal program included in the 1935 Social Security Act was called "Aid to Dependent Children," with no mention of families or mothers/parents.[2] Its original goal was to save children from orphanages. Not only were orphanages considerably more expensive than supporting dependent children within their own families, but studies had also found that orphanages were harmful to children.[3] Federal welfare was thus never focused on supporting mothers per se, but rather was adopted as a better and less expensive alternative to orphanages or foster care for dependent children in single-mother families (Katz, 1986).

Program administration of welfare also reflected this primary interest in the children. In the earlier state-level mother's pension programs, as well as in the early years of the federalized welfare program, children's welfare was central to the welfare program in several ways. In some states, the juvenile court judge was in charge of supervising welfare cases. In virtually all states, mothers were judged and given or denied cash benefits on the basis of their children's well-being, as measured by their children's grades, ability to speak English, and noncriminal behavior (Pearce, 1984). So strong was this emphasis that taking a regular job (which in the early part of the century meant 10 to 12 hours a day, 6 days a week), given the lack of acceptable child care, was considered neglect and grounds for losing benefits and having the children put in an orphanage. Doing informal work, however, such as taking in laundry or boarders, was encouraged and often necessitated by meager benefits, but only as long as it did not interfere with parenting.

With the advent of the women's movement, including the battered women's movement, welfare came to be seen in a new light by welfare rights activists. That is, for women with abusive or nonsupporting husbands, welfare is one way of achieving independence. Even so, given the meager benefits and many strings attached, the welfare system has also been characterized as "state patriarchy" (Brown, 1981) or, as welfare rights advocate Johnnie Tillmon (1976) puts it, welfare is a "a supersexist marriage. You trade in *a* man for *the* man" (p. 356).

At the same time, another consequence of the women's movement further influenced the way the welfare system viewed and treated poor women. The idea that women's primary and only role is as mothers has declined to the point that, today, most women want to and expect to work. Furthermore, because of the falling wages of male workers, many women believe that they must work for economic reasons. Not surprisingly, the welfare system now expects single mothers to assume the roles of both mother and father, of not only nurturer but also provider.

At the same time, many women who turn to welfare as a means to help them escape from abusive partners are often precisely the more traditional women who have been heavily dependent on their partners economically, with little or no experience in the paid workforce. They often are ill-prepared, psychologically or in terms of skill and experience, to move into the role of economic provider, and particularly not simultaneously with leaving their abusers. Yet, at a time of great emotional turmoil and economic need for their families, and particularly if their children have also been abused, they find themselves faced with a set of conflicting demands from the welfare and child welfare systems and with sets of difficult choices.

Choices Facing the Mother
Experiencing Domestic Violence

Going on welfare is not usually the first thing that women experiencing abuse do. Indeed, most women try first to preserve the integrity of their families, hiding their own abuse and/or that of their children. If they do seek help, they usually do so first from those whom they trust—if they have not been cut off from these sources—such as relatives, friends, and colleagues at work. Through the help of these informal networks, they may try many times to get the abusers to stop or to leave the abusers. Although those who work in the field generally believe that few abusers will ever voluntarily stop, many women do not reach this conclusion until many efforts have been made involving reconciliations and broken promises and, too often, more abuse has occurred (Pagelow, 1981; Walker, 1984). In addition, if their children are also being abused, there is even less reason to seek help formally because of the risk of losing the children. That is, women in domestic violence situations are often seen as, at best, ineffective mothers and, at worst, as incompetent and incapable of protecting their children. Thus, "domestic violence" is one of the key "risk factors" for children being placed in foster care (Mills, 1996).

Once she has exhausted whatever informal resources she has available, a woman moving toward leaving her abuser is often forced to turn to more formal aid. At this point, she is faced with two sets of issues, the first having to do with housing (whether to stay in the family home or to leave and go to a shelter or other housing), and the second with income (whether to seek welfare aid or employment or both).

Housing Issues

The housing issue presents a woman with a real Hobbesian choice. If she stays in the family home, then the abuser must leave—and stay away. The latter may require a protection order or police intervention or both, which may increase the risk of violence in retaliation and, at the least, requires the mother to be a vigilant monitor because the abuser knows exactly where she and the children are. If she leaves and goes to a shelter, conversely, *she* is now homeless and risks not being able to find housing within the constraints of the limited availability of subsidized housing, and that may mean losing her children to foster care. In short, leaving the physical home may remove the children and herself from further abuse, but at the same time it puts her family at risk for homelessness and family breakup.

The choice has further complexities. If she stays in the home, that means she, in effect, becomes the one responsible for any further abuse

that occurs to her children (as well as to herself). She may seek the aid
of the courts, in the form of a protection order, but judges are
sometimes reluctant to make the male homeless. (Because he is the
breadwinner, many view him as the owner of the home, and thus
evicting him is confiscating the house he has bought with his own
hard-earned money.) Moreover, a woman may be reluctant to bring
in the police because, whether her husband is arrested and/or removed
or not, there is a chance that turning to the authorities may escalate
the violence against herself or the children (Sherman, 1992).[4] If she
starts proceedings for divorce or official separation, then she has the
problem of supervision during his visitation with the children, custody
fights, possible kidnapping of the children, and so forth (Saunders,
1994). Nevertheless, despite the many problems, at least initially many
women choose the option of staying, with or without protection
orders forcing their abusers to stay away from home.

To leave the home with one's children usually means that the
woman becomes homeless—fairly soon, if not immediately. Most
double up with friends and family if they can, but many either have
no family or friends close by or have become cut off from them over
the time abuse was occurring. Even with much sympathy, these housing situations are often overcrowded and unstable.

Going to a shelter is also, at best, only a temporary solution. At
worst, one might be turned away because one's children are too old
(or, in some shelters, male children over a certain age are not accepted)
or there is no room. If that happens, then one is at risk of losing the
children immediately. Although adults may choose to live on the
streets, when children are homeless, it is considered a form of abuse
or neglect on the part of parents—that is, they are failing to provide
food and shelter—and as a result the children are often put in foster
care. Once they are in the custody of the state, it is difficult for a
mother to get them back because now the standard is that of the child
welfare system; that is, the mother must show that she is able to
provide food, shelter, and other necessities, as well as a nurturing
environment (having lost them because of a finding of abuse or
neglect). Given a past history of little employment or skills and low
self-esteem, obtaining employment is difficult, and now without children she is ineligible for cash aid or housing assistance. Caught in this
Catch-22—without children, she is ineligible for aid, and without
assistance, she cannot provide the housing and food necessary to
regain her children—the barriers to restoring her family are great.

Thus, a substantial but unknown portion of children in foster care are there because of these consequences (flight leading to homelessness, inadequate shelters) of domestic violence (Pearce, 1990).

Even if a woman is able to get into a shelter with her children, she is still in danger of homelessness and subsequently of losing them. Most shelters have a very short time limit, typically 30 days, not enough time to secure permanent housing or a job, much less deal with the specific issues of domestic violence and abuse. Although shelters for homeless families generally have more spaces than do battered women's shelters, the former rarely have services geared to domestic violence or abuse, although perhaps half the families coming to such shelters have experienced either or both (Zorza, 1991). General family shelters also have very short time limits.

One irony of the domestic violence movement is its inability to realize its ideals because of a chronic shortage of resources. Thus, although battered women's shelters ideally provide respite and access to services that empower women to start a new chapter in their lives, they are almost universally so strapped for funds and space that what is offered is often overcrowded and minimally adequate to the need. Meeting immediate needs, such as for food and shelter, thus often takes precedence over longer range, and ultimately more empowering, strategies such as job training, counseling, and housing assistance. As one group of authors put it, "[S]ervices for abused women remain at the fringe of the social services delivery system" (Davis, Hagen, & Early, 1994, p. 703). This chronic lack of access to resources has meant that shelters for battered women have not become part of the system. Though, perhaps, this has saved them from being co-opted and institutionalized, it has also kept them far from accomplishing their goals of providing women with services beyond emergency and stop-gap, the kind of services that would empower them to become economically self-sufficient.

Trying to secure permanent housing is very difficult. A few communities have "transitional housing," but the number of places is far less than the need. The average wait for public housing is often 1 to 2 years or even more (with enormous variation between communities), and obtaining Section 8 certificates can take even longer. Although those who are "displaced" (by a fire or domestic violence) are supposed to receive priority, they rarely do. One of the more ironic provisions is that, for those who are living in public housing at the time of separation, whoever *leaves* is considered to have abandoned the housing and thus goes back to the bottom of the waiting list—even if that means the abuser gets the housing and the mother and children become homeless.

Homeless mothers and children are somewhat at the mercy of the resources of the shelter system. The extent to which shelter workers and volunteers help families find housing depends on these helpers' perception of the readiness and ability of the family to establish an independent home. Because many women return to their abusers again and again before finally leaving, many shelter workers are unwilling to use up their limited supply of willing landlords unless they believe that a family is a good risk for succeeding. Finally, the nature of the struggle with domestic violence often leaves women without the basics to set up housing: no credit history, no landlord references, little or no income/money, often no papers at all, and not even an address if they are doubled up illegally or living in a shelter.

The stay in the shelter is a time, though often too short, for mothers to try to reestablish themselves. The shelter emphasizes safety and validation of the woman first. For this reason, shelter workers may ask a woman to not work or to quit a job because her abuser may trace her to the shelter from work, endangering not only herself but the other women as well. Unless the shelter is able to secure new employment and housing for her, she may end up more economically vulnerable than when she left her abusive partner.

Welfare and/or Work Issues

Although welfare provides an income, it is meager at best. Indeed, in many places, cash assistance is well below what rent alone requires, much less meeting other needs. This often forces families who have turned to public assistance to double up or to live in undesirable neighborhoods characterized by high levels of violence and drug abuse. In addition, with the 1996 welfare reform provisions, recipients face limits on the number of years they may receive welfare (a maximum of 5 years, and as little as 21 months in some states) and are being required to enter employment quickly. Thus, the need for income, the inadequacy and limits on benefits, and work requirements all necessitate employment, often very quickly. Priority for housing assistance, and exemptions from welfare work requirements available for victims of domestic violence, are, unfortunately, rarely available and may in some cases block access to needed services such as education and job training.

Employment particularly highlights the different perspectives of the battered women's movement, welfare, and the child welfare system. Domestic violence advocates are aware that women who have left abusers, and their children, are often quite traumatized and need intensive services to begin the healing process in those first months. The welfare system, however, does not formally recognize this issue.[5] Focused on the need to enter employment as quickly as possible, mothers are often required to engage almost immediately in a job search, and most must accept almost any job offered.

When leaving the abuser and going on welfare happen at approximately the same time, it may be especially difficult for the children, and certainly not easy for the mother. Children in particular may feel conflicted about the absence of their father, even if they have been abused, and the moves to shelters, temporary housing, new schools and neighborhoods, and/or onto assistance are further traumatizing. Even without their mother's absence for work, they may experience problems in school and other settings. Moreover, it is difficult for the mother to do well, especially if newly reentering the workforce, if she or her children are struggling with the issues of domestic violence and abuse. The welfare system's focus on work precludes dealing with these issues, whereas the child welfare system's focus on the child puts it at odds with the welfare system because a mother who is working or looking for work is often unable to protect her children, physically and emotionally, from their abuser.

Conclusion: Domestic Violence and the Welfare System

As we have seen, mothers with children who experience domestic violence are often caught in a three-way struggle among the child welfare system, the welfare (public assistance) system, and the battered women's movement's system of shelters and related services. Whereas domestic violence services seek to empower women and help them start new lives separate from their abusers, the child welfare system seeks to protect the child, and the welfare system is focused on getting the mother into employment. There are no "villains" here; each system has legitimate interests it is pursuing, yet women—and their children—are often hurt by being caught between the different perspectives and priorities of each set of services.

Under the new Temporary Assistance to Needy Families (TANF) program, which replaces AFDC, states have the option to "exempt" women experiencing domestic violence from certain requirements of the new law. Yet for many, the need is not for exemption as much as for differential treatment, one that allows healing to take place, provides housing and safety during that time, and then moves toward more permanent solutions such as job training and employment when both mothers and children are ready. It is possible to imagine these three systems working together, but a first step must be to acknowledge how current practices often subject mothers and their families to conflicting, even mutually exclusive, demands that undermine the goals of all involved, in order to move toward healing and positive family functioning.

Notes

1. Indeed, a good indicator of this contrast is in Zuravin and DePanfilis's 1997 study of factors affecting foster care placement of children—one of which is domestic violence. No characteristics of caregivers other than the mother are included because the case records used routinely lacked practically any information on anyone other than the mother.

2. In 1950, the name of the program was changed to Aid to Families With Dependent Children, or AFDC for short.

3. Younger children suffered from the "failure to thrive" syndrome—literally a lack of love—whereas older children became young criminals.

4. Evidence suggests that obtaining a protection order may lead to a temporary lessening of violence and harassment but may increase it later, 6 months or more after the initial incident that led to the protection order (Davis , Hagen, & Early, 1994).

5. The single exception is the case of those states that adopt the Family Violence Option. See Chapter 11 for a fuller discussion of this issue.

References

Brown, C. (1981). Mothers, fathers, and children: From private to public patriarchy. In L. Sargent (Ed.), *Women and revolution: A discussion of the unhappy marriage of Marxism and feminism* (pp. 239-267). Boston: South End.

Davis, L V., Hagen, J. L., & Early, T. J. (1994). Social services for battered women: Are they adequate, accessible, and appropriate? *Social Work, 39,* 695-704.

Katz, M. (1986). *In the shadow of the poorhouse: A social history of welfare in America.* New York: Basic Books.

McKay, M. M. (1994). The link between domestic violence and child abuse: Assessment and treatment considerations. *Child Welfare, 73,* 29-34.

Mills, L. (1996). Empowering battered women transnationally: The case for postmodern interventions. *Social Work, 41,* 261-268.

National Coalition Against Domestic Violence. (1991). *1991 national directory of domestic violence programs: A guide to community shelters, safe homes, and services programs.* Washington, DC: Author.

Pagelow, M. D. (1981). Factors affecting women's decisions to leave violent relationships. *Journal of Family Issues, 2,* 391-414.

Pearce, D. (1984). Farewell to alms: Women's fare under welfare. In J. Freeman (Ed.), *Women: A feminist perspective* (pp. 502-515). Palo Alto, CA: Mayfield.

Pearce, D. (1990, August). *The herstory of homelessness: A women's perspective on the housing crisis.* Paper presented at the annual meeting of the American Sociological Association, Washington, DC.

Peled, E. (1997). The battered women's movement response to children of battered women: A critical analysis. *Violence Against Women, 3,* 424-446.

Saunders, D. (1994). Custody decisions in families experiencing woman abuse. *Social Work, 39,* 51-59.

Sherman, L. W. (with Schmidt, J., & Rogan, D. P.). (1992). *Policing domestic violence: Experiments and dilemmas.* New York: Free Press.

Tillmon, J. (1976). Welfare is a women's issue. In R. Baxandall, L. Gordon, & S. Reverby (Eds.), *America's working women: A documentary history—1600 to the present* (pp. 355-358). New York: Random House.

Walker, L. (1984). *The battered woman.* New York: Springer.

Zorza, J. (1991). Woman battering: A major cause of homelessness. *Clearinghouse Review, 25,* 420-429.

Zuravin, S. J., & DePanfilis, D. (1997). Factors affecting foster care placement of children receiving child protective services. *Social Work Research, 21,* 34-42.

9

Connections Between Child Abuse and Welfare

One State's Story

Ruth A. Brandwein

This chapter focuses on the connection between child abuse and the use of public assistance. Using statistical data and case material from one state, reported by the official in charge of the state agency conducting child protective services investigations,[1] it begins to address two key questions: (a) What happens to mothers in situations in which determinations of child abuse or neglect are made when the mothers are not their children's abusers? and (b) How often and under what circumstances do these mothers turn to public assistance because of the loss of support of the abusers who have been required to leave the homes? In seeking answers to these questions, the chapter also covers how poor mothers can be victimized by the very system that is charged with protecting their children.

States do not systematically compare data from the administrative unit responsible for child protective services with the one providing public assistance, despite the fact that both functions are usually performed within the same agency. In Utah, that umbrella agency was the State of Utah Department of Human Services, and within it the Division of Child and Family Services was responsible for child protective services.[2]

Mary Noonan, director of the Child and Family Division, recalls, "It was like moving a mountain for me to find out how many . . . parents whose children come into care eventually have to apply for welfare benefits, and after some gymnastics . . . with our database, they were able to provide me the roughest of data."

During a 15-month period, from February 1995 through April 1996, child abuse was substantiated[3] in approximately 11,000 families. In 22% of these families, the custodial parent, usually the mother, had to apply for Aid to Families With Dependent Children (AFDC) within 2 months of the substantiation of child abuse and neglect. This is a telling piece of information. Over one fifth of mothers who, prior to an abuse or neglect substantiation, were not on welfare had to apply within 60 days of that determination. To understand why, a dramatically illustrative case from the files of Utah's Division of Child and Family Services is presented.

Alice's Case

Alice's[4] case was opened in the Division of Child and Family Services about 4 years ago and occurred in a northern Utah city. Alice was a 27-year-old mother of four, two girls and two boys, all under the age of 11. She was living with her second husband, the children's stepfather.

Alice was working two jobs. Her daytime job was at Kmart, and her evening job was in a fast-food shop. Her schedule required her to be away from home from about 9:30 every morning until almost 10:00 at night. All the children were in school except the youngest, who was at home. He did not attend preschool. The division became involved because the children's caretaker, the stepfather, was found to have sexually abused the two girls, who were 7 and 9 years of age. After the accusation, the children were seen at Primary Children's Medical Center, and the Division was able to substantiate abuse very quickly, within a week of the referral.

After abuse by the stepfather was substantiated, the Division staff told the mother that she had two little girls who had been

victims of sexual abuse. Staff explained that their first respon-
sibility is to protect these children and asked the mother what
she intended to do: Can you quit your job? Can you apply for
AFDC to enable you to be home during the day when the
children are not in school or in day care? Can you, and are you
willing to, have the stepfather leave?

Charges were filed against the stepfather (the perpetrator),
but the criminal proceeding had yet to play out. Meanwhile,
the mother was faced with having to develop a plan, using her
rather narrow network of friends and family, so that the two
abused children (who had been temporarily removed) could be
returned home, receive appropriate medical and mental health
therapy for the abuse they had experienced, and be protected
by her.

The stepfather, a professional, was the family's principal
breadwinner. When the mother chose to protect her children,
she asked him to move out so that the children could return
home. The children were returned to her because the stepfather
did leave the home. At that point, the situation disintegrated.
Alice's jobs both paid minimum wage. She had to quit her
evening job so that she could be at home to supervise the
children. She tried to maintain her day job for a period of time,
but within 3 months she found herself needing to apply for
public assistance. The family's financial situation deteriorated
to the point where they were evicted from their apartment.
Because they were now homeless, the Division removed all four
children.

The children were separated into two foster placements. The
two girls were placed in a home that specializes in dealing with
victims of sexual abuse. The youngest, who was under school
age, and the older boy were placed in a different foster home.
They were all living in the same city but in different neighbor-
hoods. The mother was faced with working out a service plan
to achieve her goal of return of her children.

Alice lost custody of all four of her children despite the fact
that she was not responsible in any way for the abuse that
occurred. Not only had she not participated in the abuse, but
as soon as she became apprised of it, she had immediately
cooperated with the medical professionals at the medical
center to make sure all appropriate care was provided for the

children. The only "sin" she had committed was that she had been working all day and was not at home during the day when the abuse occurred. Now she found herself with her four children gone, her second marriage in disarray, and criminal charges facing her ex-husband. Her ability to obtain adequate housing was undercut because of her loss of income.

Alice was caught in a classic double bind. The division required her to remove the perpetrator, who was the principal breadwinner from the home, and required her to give up her evening job in order to keep her children. Having done so, the ensuing loss of income led to homelessness, which resulted in the loss of her children.

Alice is an incredible person who was eventually reunited with her children. In the next 2½ years, the Division worked with her. She managed to complete her high school equivalency and then attend community college. Eventually, she was able to obtain a job that enabled her to provide minimum housing and a stable home for her children. Alice, now 34, has her children back. Nevertheless, 2½ years had passed, during which her children were in foster homes.

During their separation, she was able to work with both foster families so that she maintained an ongoing relationship with her children. She was a woman with sufficient skills to enable her to do so. She was able to obtain a bus pass, making it possible for her to visit the children. She was able to ensure that they continued to receive the mental help follow-up care they needed. She endeavored to celebrate Christmas and the children's birthdays as best she could with her family.

The family is still together. No other incident of neglect or abuse has occurred. Alice has not remarried and has worked her way off welfare. 🔰

How the System Works

Under federal law, each state is responsible for operating a Child Protective Services (CPS) program, but it is administered somewhat differently in each state. In some larger states, operational responsibility is delegated to the counties, with state oversight. In some jurisdictions, as in Utah, it is part of an umbrella human services agency, including mental health services for youths and the aging. Until 1997, it also included public assistance, which was subsequently moved to a new agency (see Note 2). In other states, CPS is part of a department that also administers public assistance but not other human services. A third model is for CPS to be part of a separate children's services department. In New York, Family and Children's Services, which is responsible for CPS, foster care, and adoptions, was recently separated into a freestanding agency, apart from public assistance. Despite specific differences in structural setting, procedures, and court organization,[5] the examples from Utah are somewhat generalizable to the rest of the nation.

When CPS receives a complaint about abuse or neglect, it is obligated to send an investigator to begin what is, in most instances, a 30-day process of determining whether sufficient evidence substantiates the alleged abuse or neglect. The determination of abuse or neglect is based on multiple factors, not the least of which is whether the perpetrator can be identified, whether who was at home at the time of the alleged neglect or abuse can be identified, and whether it can be ascertained who knew about the predicament the children were in and therefore had an opportunity to prevent the abuse or neglect.[6]

In making the determination, the CPS worker first approaches the custodial parent or parents, typically the mother. The mother often is married, with the children's father or stepfather at home, or she may have a boyfriend living in the home. Regardless of the availability of another parent, the expectation of CPS is that it is principally the mother's role to protect.

If CPS finds that abuse or neglect has been perpetrated by someone other than the mother, the worker meets with her, when possible in the context of the larger family who might be available as a resource to her. Nevertheless, the worker discusses primarily with the mother the factors leading to the abuse or neglect. She must explain how she intends to prevent future abuse or neglect and how she intends to protect the children, and CPS may offer or refer her to services to assist her. Regardless of whether the abuser is father, stepfather or boyfriend, CPS focuses on how the mother will protect the children. Among the questions to be answered are whether she will stay at home, work, or go on welfare. Availability of help from extended family may also be explored.

After the determination of abuse or neglect has been made and the assessment of the mother's ability to protect has been conducted, a decision is made whether to remove the children. If it is found that the mother is unable or incapable of protecting the children, CPS moves in to separate the family, and the children are placed in foster care or in a kinship placement. A plan is put in place for the children's future. Prior to the new Adoption and Safe Families Act of 1997 (P.L. 105-89), the existing law (Adoption Assistance and Child Welfare Act of 1980) required that the first goal was reunification and that CPS was responsible for working toward the goal in good faith. Whether or not the children are eventually returned, however, separation is an irrevocable path. Once the family has been separated and the foster care system is involved, even if the children are later returned an indelible mark has been left on the family unit.

If a child is removed and the juvenile (or family) court judge[7] upholds that decision, then the mother is faced with negotiating a "service plan" with the agency; this plan identifies the barriers she must overcome in order for the children to be returned to her.

In Utah, as in many other states, a frequent barrier is the lack of suitable housing. If, like Alice, a mother has lost substantial family income or has had to quit her job and apply for public assistance because of the abuser, her lack of suitable housing and inability to have her children returned may have been caused by the CPS requirements. To satisfy the juvenile court judge that the children can be safely returned, the service plan may require her to secure employment and demonstrate that she can financially support the children. Yet, the requirement that she be at home to supervise them may make it impossible for her to be employed at a level where she can demonstrate financial viability. In many parts of the country, housing costs may exceed the entire public assistance grant.[8]

The service plan may also require that the mother obtain appropriate mental and physical health services for the family. She is also expected to visit her children regularly while they are in foster care. This means she has to negotiate the system of arranging for services, transportation to and from the services, and transportation to visit them.[9] Yet, on a limited income she may not be able to maintain reliable private transportation, and many rural and suburban areas lack adequate public transportation.

As discussed in the previous chapter, the CPS system, in its effort to protect children, may treat mothers as adversaries, rather than enlist them as part of a team to help and protect the children. Financial obstacles facing the mother because of her need to be available to supervise her children may require her, like Alice, to seek public assistance. Yet, the low levels of assistance and the stigmatization of recipients may jeopardize her chances of keeping her children. If the children are removed, she is no longer eligible for AFDC. If she loses AFDC or even if she is on it, her lack of adequate income and housing may stymie her efforts to have her children returned once they have been removed.

New Child Welfare Reform Legislation and the Personal Responsibility Act

It is perhaps more than coincidental that the Adoption and Safe Families Act of 1997 (P.L. 105-89), together with the Personal Responsibility and Work Opportunity Reconciliation Act of 1996 (PRA; P.L. 104-193), were both passed recently by Congress.[10] Whether intended or unintended, the effects of both are to punish and demonize women, particularly poor women. Other chapters of this book discuss in detail the provisions and impact of the PRA. In brief, it imposes a 5-year lifetime limit for receipt of public assistance and has strict work requirements. The newly passed Adoption and Safe Families Act reduces the length of time that children may remain in foster care prior to being freed for adoption. It also changes the primary goal from family preservation to "the best interests of the child."

The new act has many positive features. It was formulated in reaction to some serious negative consequences resulting from implementation of the previous law (Adoption and Child Welfare Act of 1980). It encourages adoption, simplifying the process and providing additional incentives, and reduces the time for implementation of a child's permanency plan. Under the old legislation, children were not to remain in foster care longer than 30 months, but in fact many languished in care, shuttled from one foster home to another, for the better part of their childhoods. Because the primary goal was reunification of families, parents (most often mothers) were given every chance for rehabilitation. After the use of crack became endemic, it became clear that seriously addicted crack parents had little hope of rehabilitation and that their children were being denied the opportunity of a permanent, stable new home.

The 1997 Act shortens the time frame for a child's first permanency hearing from 18 to 12 months and sets new requirements for the state to petition for termination of parental rights. Termination must be initiated after a child has been in foster care for 15 of the most recent 22 months (National Association of Social Workers, 1997). This means that if a child is removed and the parent (usually the mother) who has lost custody does not comply with the plan developed by CPS and approved by the court within this time period, she will lose her parental rights. Rather than keep the children in foster care if they cannot be returned to her and extend the time for her to comply with the service plan, CPS will free the children for adoption and she will lose them permanently.

Although the purpose of the law is to achieve permanency for children, ensuring that they do not spend their childhoods shuttling from foster home to foster home, the backlash against inordinately long stays in foster care has a severely negative effect on the relationship between children and their mothers. In Alice's case, if the new law had been in effect, rather than being able to regain custody of her children after the 2 ½ years it took her to work her way off welfare, she could have lost them forever.

If Alice's case had occurred after the PRA went into effect, she would not have been helped to complete her high school equivalency and take college courses. This education eventually enabled her to gain employment that paid her enough to support her children. Under the PRA, she would have been required to either find any low-paying job available or remain on public assistance while working off her grant in a workfare setting. She would not have been able to complete her education and qualify for a higher-paid job.

If another Alice has similar problems with child protective services in the future and she has already received public assistance for a total of 5 years, she will not even be able to receive assistance. Will she remain with her children's abuser for financial support? If so, she would lose custody of her children. If she left him but could not make a home for the children within 15 months, she could lose her children. Under the new law, another Alice in similar circumstances will have little chance of having her family reunited.

Summary

From the Utah records, it appears that many women who are not abusers themselves are forced to turn to public assistance when CPS has determined that their children have been abused or neglected. It is not known how many women nationwide have become welfare recipients as a result of CPS abuse and neglect determinations. Further research is necessary to determine whether the Utah figure of over 20% of such women turning to public assistance is representative.

What is known is that the very requirements and expectations that a mother must be the protector of her children may make it necessary for her to seek financial aid. Even when she has done nothing wrong, because she is expected to protect the children, she may temporarily lose custody of them. With the new laws shortening the time period by which she must fulfill the court's service plan and the new restrictions on public assistance, she is caught in a vise. She may need public assistance so that she is not dependent financially on her children's abuser. She may need public assistance so that she can be at home to provide proper supervision and fulfill her expected role as their protector. The new PRA regulations, however, may make it impossible for her to receive public assistance.

If it were determined that large numbers of welfare recipients were in that position because they were trying to protect their children from abuse or neglect, perhaps policymakers, public officials, and the public would reconsider their negative views of public assistance and reconsider support for educational provisions. Otherwise, the PRA may unnecessarily break up families and deprive children of their mothers' care.

Notes

1. Statistical data and case materials from Utah were drawn from the transcript of a presentation by Mary Noonan, J.D., then director of the Children and Families Services Division of the State of Utah Department of Human Services, at a national symposium, "Family Violence and Welfare: What Are the Links," sponsored by the Spafford Endowed Chair at the University of Utah Graduate School of Social Work, Salt Lake City, May 21, 1996.

2. In July 1997, Utah established a new Department of Workfare Services. Effective July 1, 1997, the Office of Family Support, which is responsible for public assistance, was relocated from the Department of Human Services to a separate Department of Workfare Services. Child and Family Services remained in the Department of Human Services.

3. In some states, the term *substantiated* is used; in others, *indicated* is the term used to mean that the charge of child abuse was proved after an investigation. Between one third and two thirds of all child abuse charges, depending on the jurisdiction, are not substantiated (or not indicated) after the required investigation period. No official

determination of abuse does not necessarily mean no abuse has occurred; rather, the investigation was unable to uncover sufficient evidence to substantiate such a charge in court. In many cases, abuse has clearly occurred but it is not possible to determine the perpetrator. In other cases, such as sexual abuse with young children, a child may be unable to testify and physical evidence may be insufficient. In physical abuse, it is sometimes not possible to determine whether the injury was caused accidentally or deliberately.

4. Client name has been changed to maintain confidentiality.

5. Although Child Protective Services investigations and determinations are conducted by an agency under the executive branch of local or state government, the courts have jurisdiction for making the final decision to remove a child from his or her parent's custody. The CPS agency must go to court and make its case in an adversarial process against the parent.

6. In Utah, "dependency" is an additional complaint category, and the identity of the perpetrator is not always a necessary focus of the investigation (M. Noonan, personal correspondence, March 5, 1998).

7. In Utah, these decisions are made in juvenile court; in New York, in family court. In most states, it is usually in one of these two. In Utah, in about 94% of cases in which a child is removed, the juvenile court agrees with that decision and the children remain in care. This pattern varies widely. In Suffolk County, New York, family court judges are more protective of the biological family, and family law attorneys more aggressively challenge CPS. Often, a parent can be persuaded to "voluntarily surrender" custody. When a parent does not, it is much more difficult for CPS, in that venue, to persuade the judge to remove the children or, if there has been a temporary removal by CPS, to honor that decision and keep the children in custody.

8. For example, in Suffolk County, the monthly average market rate for renting a two-bedroom house was $850, yet the housing grant was only $422 monthly and the entire grant was less than $600.

9. In New York, the CPS agency is required to provide the cost of transportation for a mother visiting her children if she is unable to afford it. The foster parents may be required to provide the health services necessary for the children while in their care.

10. Foreshadowing this national legislation, in 1994 the Utah state legislature, in response to a state audit that found serious flaws in the Utah child welfare system, passed sweeping legislation shortening the time allowed before a child could be freed for adoption.

References

Adoption and Safe Families Act of 1997, Pub. L. 105-89 (November 19, 1997).
Adoption Assistance and Child Welfare Act of 1980, Pub. L. 96-272 (June 17, 1980).
National Association of Social Workers. (1997, December). *Government relations update: Adoption and Safe Families Act of 1997 (H.R. 867) Public law 105-89.* Washington, DC: Author.
Personal Responsibility and Work Reconciliation Act of 1996, Pub. L. 104-193, 110 Stat. 2105 (August 22, 1996).

10

Childhood Sexual Abuse

The Forgotten Issue in Adolescent Pregnancy and Welfare Reform

Debra Boyer

The political debate on welfare reform often targets adolescent pregnancy as the primary cause of expanding welfare costs. It has been politically expedient to simplify the relationship between adolescent pregnancy and welfare, which may not be fully understood until "welfare to work" programs are carefully evaluated. Successful social policy in this area will require a more complex analysis of the nature of both adolescent pregnancy and welfare dependency. Childhood sexual abuse is a factor that has long been ignored in the etiology of adolescent pregnancy, and as I argue in this chapter, abuse may have significant repercussions for welfare reform programs.

Adolescent Pregnancy and Welfare

Adolescent pregnancy has been represented to the public as a contemporary phenomenon of "epidemic" proportions. The number of births to teenagers, however, has actually decreased: In 1970, 656,000 teenage women had babies, compared with 533,000 in 1990 (U.S. Department of Commerce, 1993, p. 74). Adolescent pregnancy has been construed as a social problem partially because of the increase in out-of-wedlock births among teenagers, which account for about 70% of all teenage births. Although the increase in out-of-wedlock births among teenagers is cause for concern, this increase should be viewed from the broader context of changing reproductive patterns within the whole of society. Three quarters of unintended pregnancies occur to women age 20 and older. Teenagers account for a much smaller proportion of out-of-wedlock births today than in decades past (Alan Guttmacher Institute [AGI], 1995).

Teenagers are involved in the problems of unintended and out-of-wedlock pregnancies, but both teenagers and adults have been caught by the same shifting economic structures that challenge family structure and influence reproductive patterns. Adolescent pregnancy can only be understood in relation to social and economic forces that influence childbearing practices among all women. These are not issues understood or resolved by a singular focus on adolescent pregnancy.

The correlation of adolescent pregnancy to the "welfare problem" is equally confounded and often misrepresented as well. The number of families on Aid to Families With Dependent Children (AFDC) increased 163%, from two to five million, between 1970 and 1993 (AGI, 1995). Of the 3.8 million mothers aged 15 to 44 who were AFDC recipients in 1993, 55% became mothers when they were teenagers. In 1993, many recipients were not teenage mothers, and never-married women receiving AFDC are less likely to be current or former teenage mothers now than they were in the 1970s. Reports prepared by the Alan Guttmacher Institute further show that the growth in never-married women who are mothers continues to be more pronounced among women who are not welfare recipients.

The information cited above points to a decisive shift in childbearing patterns among teenage and adult women who are both inside and outside the welfare system. Significant numbers of women who begin childbearing in their teenage years, however, do end up on welfare. About three fourths of unmarried adolescent mothers begin receiving welfare within 5 years of the birth of their first child (AGI, 1995). These mothers face the same problems of other single mothers in our society: child care, health insurance, emotional support, financial

assistance, and adequate employment opportunities. It is crucial that
these issues are addressed in welfare reform because of the additional
obstacles faced by women who become mothers in their teenage years
and receive welfare. These women are generally poorer, less educated,
and less likely than non-teenage mothers to receive financial assistance
from relatives or their children's father.

A more complicated picture begins to emerge the closer one looks
at all the factors that characterize pregnant and parenting adolescents.
Successful welfare reform depends on a thorough understanding of
the causes of teenage pregnancy and the often ignored barriers faced
by these young women. Among these issues are trauma histories and
the long-term effects of childhood maltreatment.

Childhood Sexual Abuse and Adolescent Pregnancy

Significant numbers of adolescents who become pregnant have
histories of childhood sexual abuse (Boyer & Fine, 1992; Butler &
Burton, 1990; Gershenson et al., 1989). A survey conducted by the
Ounce of Prevention Fund of 445 black, white, and Hispanic pregnant
and parenting adolescents indicated that 61% reported sexual abuse.
Of those who reported abuse, 65% had been abused by more than one
perpetrator and 50% had more than one experience of abuse. A later
study conducted by Boyer and Fine (1992) in Washington state reported that two thirds of 535 pregnant and parenting adolescents had
been sexually abused prior to their first pregnancies: 55% had been
molested, 42% had been victims of attempted rape, and 44% had been
raped. On average, respondents in the Boyer and Fine study were 9.7
years old at first molestation, with 24% reporting their first such
experience occurring at age 5 or younger. The mean age of the
offender was 27.4 years. Of the victims, 77% were molested more
than once, and 54% were victimized by a family member. The average
age at first rape was 13.3 years for victims and 22.6 years for
perpetrators. One half of the respondents who had been raped were
raped more than once. The prevalence of abuse in the Boyer and Fine
sample is higher than estimates made for general populations. In
Russell's (1986) study of 900 women selected at random, one out of
three reported some form of sexual exploitation, and one out of four
reported rape. Finkelhor, Hotaling, Lewis, and Smith (1990) reported

that 27% of women surveyed had experienced sexual abuse before age 18.

Sexual Abuse and High-Risk Behavior

Sexual abuse has been associated with high-risk sexual behavior and other negative outcomes for adolescent and adult women (Polit, White, & Morton, 1990; Stevens & Reicher, 1994). A comparison of abused and nonabused adolescents in the Boyer and Fine study (1992) showed that young women who had been sexually victimized before their first pregnancies also began "voluntary" intercourse earlier and were more likely than nonvictims to have used drugs and alcohol. Their sexual partners were older and more likely to be using drugs and alcohol at intercourse. The age of first pregnancy was the same for young women in both groups. Among the abused, however, partners were older.

Strong trends among the abused group showed that they were less likely to use contraception at any time and to have had an abortion. The strongest predictor for repeat pregnancy was prior abuse. Pregnant and parenting adolescents who had been abused tended to have been in violent relationships with partners in which they had been hit, slapped, or beaten or were currently being abused. Not surprisingly, women in the abused group reported more emotional abuse and physical maltreatment in childhood.

A follow-up survey of 59% of the Boyer and Fine sample revealed significant differences between the abused and nonabused group 1 year later. Adolescent parents who had been abused were more likely to have experienced repeated sexual victimization, a sexually transmitted disease, and drug and alcohol problems in the past year. The abused group was more likely to have had three or more pregnancies, and this finding held across age and race categories. The abused were more likely to be parenting two or more children, to have had Child Protective Services (CPS) contact with their children, and to have had children taken from them by CPS. One year later, the abused young women were more likely to have lower self-esteem, lower satisfaction with social relationships, lower empathy with their children, and more problems dealing with daily life tasks. No differences were found between the prepregnancy abuse and no-abuse groups on marital status, race, employment, or age in the follow-up sample (Boyer & Fine, 1992).

Childhood Abuse and Welfare Dependency

The high-risk behaviors associated with childhood maltreatment and adolescent pregnancy suggest a population that may be characterized as unprepared for self-sufficiency in many respects. The association between childhood abuse and adolescent pregnancy reported by Boyer and Fine (1992) led researchers conducting a 5-year Family Income Study in Washington State to examine childhood abuse in addition to factors traditionally associated with labor market success (Roper & Weeks, 1993). Washington State is comparable to the nation in that 52% of women on public assistance were found to have been teenage mothers (Webster & D'Allessandro, 1991). Data collected by Roper and Weeks (1993), based on telephone and face-to-face interviews with women on public assistance, indicated that 38% of women had been sexually abused while growing up. Of the public assistance sample, 20% reported sexual abuse, 18% reported sexual and physical abuse, and 9% reported physical abuse only. The prevalence of abuse among this population of women on public assistance is also higher than has been found in national studies of child abuse. The median age of first sexual abuse among women in the Family Income Study was 8, compared with the national median age of 9.6 (Finkelhor et al., 1990).

Researchers on the Family Income Study concluded that the high prevalence of abuse in relation to early sexual activity, dropping out of school, and teenage pregnancy and childbirth suggested a causal relationship and a pattern of behavior leading to welfare dependency. Women receiving welfare in Washington who were sexually abused as children had an elevated risk of early sexual activity, pregnancy in adolescence, and adolescent motherhood: 91% of women receiving welfare who were sexually abused and sexually active before age 15 had become pregnant as teenagers; 71% of women who were sexually active at an early age dropped out of school, and of those who dropped out, 93% became pregnant as teenagers (Roper & Weeks, 1993).

Roper and Weeks (1993) summarized the policy implications of their findings by noting that programs or policies directed toward preventing and mitigating the effects of childhood abuse may also influence early sexual activity, dropping out of school, teenage pregnancy and childbirth, and ultimately welfare dependency. An empirical link can be made between childhood maltreatment and welfare dependency, although more specific studies need to be conducted. It is equally important for researchers and policymakers to understand why welfare dependency may be linked with early maltreatment.

Long-term Effects of Abuse

Many negative outcomes associated with adolescent pregnancy can be interpreted as long-term sequelae of childhood maltreatment. Children who have experienced serious and uncontrollable events in their lives, such as abuse, may be affected over time and demonstrate motivational, developmental, cognitive, and emotional deficits. The clinical literature on child abuse reports such long-term effects as psychiatric illness, depression, anxiety, suicide ideation, negative sexual esteem and sexual maladjustment, drug addiction, and repeated victimization. Victims of sexual abuse are generally at high risk of problems of mental health and social functioning arising from the powerlessness and stigmatization of the abuse process (Briere, 1992; Browne & Finkelhor, 1986; Conte & Schuerman, 1987; Finkelhor & Browne, 1985).

As Putnam and Trickett (1993) have pointed out, the long-term effects of child sexual abuse are quite divergent. These researchers suggest that the psychological effects of abuse may be manifest in five interrelated areas: (a) development of self-esteem and self-concepts; (b) beliefs about personal power, control, and self-efficacy; (c) development of cognitive and social competencies; (d) emotional and behavioral regulation; and (e) psychiatric symptomatology. This schema is particularly useful for understanding the difficulty with interpersonal relations found among adolescent parents with abuse histories.

The *learned helplessness model* is useful for understanding the passive reaction of many victims of sexual abuse in relationships. The thesis put forward by Peterson and Seligman (1983) suggests that learned helplessness is a maladaptive response to victimization. The "uncontrollability" of the original abuse and repeated violations of personal boundaries is crucial for the development of subsequent interpersonal deficits.

To gain mastery over one's environment is an innate drive in all humans. Abuse and neglect in childhood can undercut the developing sense of self-efficacy. Survivors of abuse generally never gain a sense of control because their needs were often not met in predictable ways. The world is a series of random events in which they are powerless. They fail to learn the fundamental relationship of cause and effect, the basis for a sense of self-efficacy, and ultimately self-esteem. In this condition of learned helplessness, survivors have little opportunity to practice decision making, problem solving, or the other skills learned in normal social interactions.

Problems in the interpersonal domain faced by young mothers with a history of abuse are generalized to school and, importantly, to work settings and interactions. Coping strategies and defensive mechanisms used to regulate anxiety, fear, and danger such as dissociation, denial, and repression are often misinterpreted in these settings.

Impact of Sexual Abuse on Welfare Dependency

Adolescent childbearing and parenting have long been associated with significant negative economic and educational outcomes (Furstenberg, Brooks-Gunn, & Morgan, 1987; Horowitz, Klerman, Sung Kuo, & Jekel, 1991). Furstenberg et al. (1987) examined variables related to success and well-being of adolescent parents in a 17-year follow-up on 322 families (80% of the original sample first interviewed between 1986 and 1988). *Positive outcomes* were defined as educational success and economic independence. Furstenberg et al. also defined two well-being indicators—economic status and fertility. Adolescent parents who had more economic security and better educated parents were, not surprisingly, more likely to succeed. Higher educational performance at the time they gave birth was also related to success, as was fertility control. Those with lower academic achievement were more likely to be experiencing economic hardship, including being on welfare at the follow-up. They were also more likely to be unmarried and to have had additional children within 5 years of the first birth.

A clear distinction was found between those who controlled fertility and those who did not: Subsequent fertility lowered chances of success. In Furstenberg et al.'s (1987) study, 61% of additional births occurred within 5 years after the first birth. Surprisingly, 57%

had been sterilized. Of those who were not sterilized, only one fifth were reliable users of contraception. Those who were not using birth control were more likely to be receiving public assistance.

Childhood maltreatment was not a variable examined in Fursten-berg et al.'s (1987) study. It is known from later studies, however, discussed previously, that sexual abuse was related to several variables associated with negative outcomes in the Furstenberg et al. study, including use of contraception, fertility, and educational achievement. Variables associated with success in the outcome studies included (a) amount of schooling prior to pregnancy, (b) life skills program partici-pation, (c) a sense of control, (d) low social isolation, (e) fertility control, (f) program interventions, and (g) self-efficacy. Both studies recognized a high-risk group who continued to have problems throughout their lives and who would require more intensive services for their broader needs. These success factors clearly reflect the risk factors identified in the Washington State Family Income Study (Roper & Weeks, 1993) and the Boyer and Fine study (1992) that were associated with negative outcomes among teenage parents and child-hood sexual victimization. The success variables sense of control, social isolation, fertility control, and self-efficacy are of particular interest, given what is now known about the prevalence of prior sexual abuse among adolescent parents.

Implications for Welfare Reform

Welfare reform has focused on denial of benefits to unmarried teenage mothers under age 18, a ban on additional benefits for women who have more children, employment training, and work require-ments. The long-term sequelae of sexual abuse severely challenge these goals on several fronts. For many welfare recipients who became pregnant in adolescence, a history of physical and sexual maltreatment may have disrupted their developmental processes and undermined their basic competencies. These failures may be compounded by the inability of victimized young women to comprehend and make deci-sions about increasingly complex situations and will be manifest in fertility control and employment success. It is important to examine and accommodate all factors that may affect a person's ability to leave welfare and take advantage of education and training opportunities.

Research on the psychological and emotional effects of child abuse demonstrates evidence of long-term effects in these interrelated areas: (a) self-esteem and self-concepts, (b) beliefs about personal power, control, and self-efficacy, (c) development of cognitive and social competencies, (d) emotional and behavioral regulation, and (e) psychiatric symptomatology (Putnam & Trickett, 1993). Far less attention has been paid to the impact of abuse on sensory, motor, and physical development, which underlies the more complex social and emotional functioning (Trickett & McBride-Chang, 1995). Clinical and research literature on abuse and trauma supports the notion that labor market success may be affected by the long-term effects that child abuse may have on developmental competencies and current coping and functioning skills, as well as emotional and psychological effects. Welfare-to-work programs should address concurrent problems associated with developmental and functional deficits.

Part of my ongoing work is evaluation of a demonstration project (The Working Zone) in Seattle, Washington, that employs homeless youths and includes occupational therapy assessment and intervention (Kannenberg & Boyer, 1997).[1] Data from this project are relevant to the topic of this chapter because of the focus on employment and the prevalence of abuse among street youths (Boyer, 1989; Boyer & James, 1983; McCarthy & Hagan, 1992; McCormack, Janus, & Burgess, 1986; Yates, MacKenzie, & Pembridge, 1988). Services for high-risk adolescents, such as employment programs, much like welfare populations, are likely to have a large proportion of clients with trauma histories.

The *employment program model* is based on a developmental or occupational behavioral frame of reference (Mosey, 1981). Young people are viewed as moving through a sequence of developmental states in different areas of human function. Normal development is orderly, predictable, sequential, and cumulative and evolves by building on previous skill acquisitions. The ability to work is often expected as part of adult functioning. People with physical, developmental, or emotional disorders, however, often do not have the foundation of skills necessary to succeed at these tasks (Colman, 1975; Howard, 1986). We have found that homeless youths, as do other groups with abuse histories, lack normal play experiences and have not had control over their environments. These elements are crucial for their developing a sense of mastery. They have often failed to acquire critical skills that are normally developed in nonabusive homes through natural developmental processes (Kannenberg & Boyer, 1997).

The basic skill building assumed to be present in welfare recipients with child abuse histories may simply just not be there. In the transition from childhood to adulthood, an individual undergoes several important processes that affect employability in later life. For example, children learn to work through a sequential process beginning in exploratory play. The abused child is often robbed of childhood play, curiosity, and exploration of the environment. Adapting to fear limits learning about abilities and limitations. An abusive environment interferes with interpersonal behaviors and skill building necessary for development.

An occupational therapy screening process has been developed and successfully implemented in the employment project (The Working Zone). The occupational therapy screening consists of structured observations, a brief vocational history, and the Jacobs Prevocational Skills Assessment (JPSA; Jacobs, 1991). The JPSA consists of up to 15 tasks involving functional ability in the following skill areas necessary for successful work performance: fine motor coordination, eye-hand coordination, motor planning, attention to detail, sorting, classification and sequencing, decision-making, problem solving, organizational skills, use of tools, ability to follow directions, conceptual skills, task focus, practical daily living knowledge, and work attitudes and behaviors.

Work is underway to summarize assessment data on youths seen by both occupational therapists who have worked in the program. Preliminary assessment data on 22 youths completed by occupational therapists indicate that functional deficits tend to fall into five categories: (a) ability to follow directions, (b) ability to stay on a task, (c) ability to problem-solve, (d) ability to attend to detail, and (e) general work attitude and behavior. These problems can severely compromise employability and employment success. The desired outcome of identification and intervention with developmental deficits and significant functional problems in a social service setting is to help homeless youths enhance their ability to adjust and meet the demands of the social and work environments. These are issues I suggest should be addressed in any welfare reform program, given the probable similarities of the populations.

Many women receiving welfare have had jobs. Although they may not have maintained economic self-sufficiency for many reasons, interpersonal and developmental skill deficits arising from traumatic histories must also be accommodated. Assessments and strategies for promoting functional competencies among women on welfare are not generally included in the program designs. The positive effects of counseling, training, and other services may not be maintained because they do not address underlying developmental issues and other trauma-related problems. The developmental lags in sensory motor, cognitive, and psychosocial domains may lead to failures for women who are given opportunities for training and work; they may still not be able to make decisions, solve problems, or think logically despite services provided to them. Addressing the deficits arising from trauma is an important component for welfare-to-work programs.

Perhaps a better understanding of how early trauma affects the abilities of some young unwed mothers to learn and sustain employment may help reduce stigma. The focus should be on assessment and services to enhance functioning, rather than on blame. A word of caution, though, is important: Care must be taken not to label all young unwed mothers as functionally impaired; to do so could generate yet another type of stereotype and stigma.

Note

1. The Working Zone project evaluation is a component of Positive Options for Youth, funded by the King County Department of Children and Family Services, Seattle, Washington.

References

Alan Guttmacher Institute (AGI). (1995, February). Teenage pregnancy and the welfare reform debate. *Family Planning Perspectives, 21,* 82-85.

Boyer, D. (1989). Male prostitution and homosexual identity. *Journal of Homosexuality, 17,* 1-4.

Boyer, D., & Fine, D. (1992). Sexual abuse as a factor in adolescent pregnancy and child maltreatment. *Family Planning Perspectives, 24*(1), 4-11.

Boyer, D., & James, J. (1983). Sex and social order: The prostitute as victim. In D. MacNamara & A. Karmen (Eds.), *Victims and victimizers* (Sage Annual Review of Studies in Deviance, Vol. 7). Beverly Hills, CA: Sage.

Briere, J. (1992). *Child abuse trauma: Theory and treatment of lasting effects.* Newbury Park, CA: Sage.

Browne, A., & Finkelhor, D. (1986). Impact of child sexual abuse: A review of research. *Psychology Bulletin, 99,* 66-77.

Butler, J., & Burton, L. (1990). Rethinking teenage childbearing: Is sexual abuse a missing link? *Family Relations, 39*(1), 73-80.

Colman, W. (1975). Occupational therapy and child abuse. *American Journal of Occupational Therapy, 29*(7), 412-417.

Conte, J. A., & Schuerman, J. R. (1987). Factors associated with an increased impact of child sexual abuse. *Child Abuse and Neglect, 11,* 201-211.

Finkelhor, D., & Browne, A. (1985). The traumatic impact of child sexual abuse: A conceptualization. *American Journal of Orthopsychiatry, 55,* 530-541.

Finkelhor, D., Hotaling, G., Lewis, I. A., & Smith, C. (1990). Sexual abuse in a national survey of adult men and women: Prevalence, characteristics, and risk factors. *Child Abuse & Neglect, 14*(1), 19-28.

Furstenberg, F. F., Jr., Brooks-Gunn, J., & Morgan, S. P. (1987). Adolescent mothers and their children in later life. *Family Planning Perspectives, 19*(4), 142-252.

Gershenson, H., Musick, J., Ruch-Ross, H., Magee, V., Rubino, K., & Rosenberg, D. (1989). The prevalence of coercive sexual experience among teenage mothers. *Journal of Interpersonal Violence, 4*(2), 204-219.

Horowitz, S. M., Klerman, L. V., Sung Kuo, H., & Jekel, J. F. (1991). School-age mothers: Predictors of long-term educational and economic outcomes. *Pediatrics, 87*(6), 862-868.

Howard, A. (1986). Developmental play ages of physically abused and nonabused children. *American Journal of Occupational Therapy, 40*(10), 691-695.

Jacobs, K. (1991). Work-related programs for children and adolescents. In *Occupational therapy: Work-related programs and assessments.* Boston: Little, Brown.

Kannenberg, K., & Boyer, D. (1997). Occupational therapy evaluation and intervention in an employment program for homeless youths. *Psychiatric Services, 48*(5), 631-633.

McCarthy, B., & Hagan, J. (1992). Surviving on the street: The experiences of homeless youth. *Journal of Adolescent Research, 7*(4), 412-430.

McCormack, A., Janus, M., & Burgess, A. (1986). Runaway youths and sexual victimization: Gender differences in an adolescent runaway population. *Child Abuse and Neglect, 13,* 417-426.

Mosey, A. C. (1981). *Occupational therapy: Configurations of a profession.* New York: Raven.

Peterson, C., & Seligman, M. E. P. (1983). Learned helplessness and victimization. *Journal of Social Issues, 2,* 103-116.

Polit, D. F., White, C. M., & Morton, T. D. (1990). Child sexual abuse and premarital intercourse among high-risk adolescents. *Journal of Adolescent Health Care, 11,* 231-234.

Putnam, F., & Trickett, P. (1993). Child sexual abuse: A model of chronic trauma. *Psychiatry, 56,* 82-95.

Roper, P., & Weeks, G. (1993). *Child abuse, teenage pregnancy, and welfare dependency: Is there a link?* Olympia: Washington State Institute for Public Policy.

Russell, D. E. H. (1986). *The secret trauma: Incest in the lives of girls and women.* New York: Basis Books.

Stevens, S. C., & Reichert, S. (1994). Sexual abuse, adolescent pregnancy, and child abuse: A developmental approach to an intergenerational cycle. *Archives of Pediatric Adolescent Medicine, 148*(1), 23-27.

Trickett, P., & McBride-Chang, C. (1995). The developmental impact of different forms of child abuse and neglect. *Developmental Review, 15*(3), 311-337.

U.S. Department of Commerce. (1993). Vital statistics: Births and birth rates 1970-90. In *Statistical abstract of the United States.* Washington, DC: Government Printing Office.

Webster, C., & D'Allessandro, F. (1991). *Teenage mothers: A life of poverty and welfare?* Olympia: Washington State Institute for Public Policy.

Yates, G., MacKenzie, R., & Pembridge, J. (1988). A risk profile of runaway and non-runaway youth. *American Journal of Public Health, 78,* 820-821.

PART IV

CONCLUSION

11

Family Violence and Social Policy

Welfare "Reform" and Beyond

Ruth A. Brandwein

This book has examined the nexus between family violence, including both partner and child abuse, and the need for public assistance. The awareness of linkages between the two has been sharpened by the recent change in federal welfare law. In this final chapter, the focus is on the policy implications of the new federal and related state laws, known collectively as "welfare reform," how it may affect victims of family violence, and specific problems in implementing the new welfare provisions and concludes with a vision of what real reform would look like.

Implications of the New Welfare Law

Five-Year Lifetime Limit

As discussed earlier in this book, a lifetime limit of 60 cumulative months, or a total of 5 years, has been established as the federal

147

maximum for receipt of public assistance under the new welfare "reform" legislation (Personal Responsibility and Work Opportunity Reconciliation Act of 1996 [PRA]), but states may choose shorter time limits. They could also establish longer time limits or no limits, but federal funding available to states through the PRA could not be used after that 5-year cutoff. To date, 21 states ("Welfare Law Cuts Hundreds," 1997) have opted for a time period of less than 5 years. Utah, for example, has imposed a lifetime limit of 3 years; Connecticut, 21 months; and Texas, with the shortest limit in the nation, 18 months.

This means that if a women needs public assistance, she will be required to get her life in order, become job-ready, and obtain transportation and child care to enable her to work within that time period. Should she later lose her job and need assistance a second time, she would be unable to obtain it if she had already used up her total time.

If states choose to provide assistance beyond the 5-year maximum, they would have to fund it through state revenues. The federal law does allow states to provide exemptions from the 5-year time limit, however, for up to 20% of its total caseload. This would include those women with physical or mental disabilities (not great enough to qualify them for Supplemental Security Income [SSI], the federal disability program), those with disabled children requiring their presence at home, women in drug and alcohol recovery programs, and those with borderline mental capacities making it difficult for them to sustain employment.

A common pattern of welfare use is "cycling" (Spalter-Roth, Hartmann, & Andrews, 1992). Whereas some women stay on welfare for long periods, the more common pattern, for about 50% of welfare recipients, is a brief stay of 1 to 2 years. Many of these women, however, return one or more times while their children are young (Bane & Ellwood, 1983; Ellwood, 1988; Ruggles, 1989; Shea, 1992). For some, it is when they have another child and are unable to work. For many, it is because they have low educational attainment and can find work only in the secondary labor market.[1] Fully half the women on public assistance have not even completed high school. Another 30% have completed high school but have no further education. Even among high school graduates, the level of functional illiteracy in the United States is alarming.

What kinds of jobs are available to such women? Cashiering at Wal-Mart or the local supermarket, fast-food preparation, waitressing, unskilled assembly work, telephone solicitation, or working as a domestic are the most common. These jobs often provide no medical benefits, no paid sick leave, and no vacation time. Moreover, they are often part-time or temporary. The average woman leaving welfare for a job stays at that job for only 3 months. She may be laid off because business is slow or the small company goes out of business, completes a contract, or moves. If her car breaks down or her child becomes ill, she may not be able to get to work and so may lose her job.

Typically, these jobs pay minimum wage or slightly above minimum. At the current federal minimum wage of $5.25 per hour, a woman working 40 hours per week will earn $210, or about $900 per month. If she works 50 weeks of the year, she will have earned $10,500. The 1997 poverty level for a family of three was $13,330[2] (U.S. Department of Health and Human Services [DHHS], 1997b). In many urban communities, housing alone can cost more than $700 a month. Child care for one child can be more than $400 each month, more in a certified child care center with educational stimulation. And then the woman has a car to maintain, gasoline to get her to work and the children to child care, telephone and utilities, and other job-related expenses.

Unless a woman is able to prepare herself to qualify for a higher-paying job, she simply cannot make it. This is why so many women rotate back to welfare after short stints in the job market. In the past, these women who lost their jobs or just could not make ends meet with child care and other work-related expenses, whose children became ill, or who lost their means of transportation to work could return to the welfare rolls. After another stint, they might find another job and start the process again. Contrary to popular myth, most women on welfare have had exposure to the labor market (Spalter-Roth et al., 1992). What is remarkable is not that they are not working, but rather how many times they have tried to make it on their own at what appears to be a Sisyphean task. They keep trying in the face of almost insurmountable obstacles.

Work Provisions

In addition to the 5-year lifetime limit for receipt of cash assistance, the new federal law requires recipients to be working after just 2 years. Those who are not may be dropped from the rolls. An even harsher provision requires parents receiving assistance to participate in a community service or work experience program within just 2 months of receiving assistance. Most often, this will be workfare. Postsecondary education is no longer considered an allowable activity, and vocational training is allowed for a maximum of only 12 months.

In the first year of the law, 1997, a minimum of 25% of single parents in the total caseload were required to be in a work experience program for a minimum of 20 hours per week. By law, these figures steadily increase so that, by 2002, the last year of the act, 50% of single parents will be required to work for a minimum of 30 hours per week. States that do not meet these goals will be sanctioned with a loss of federal funds.

Workfare assignments may be in governmental or nonprofit agencies, and states may also opt to include workfare placements in the for-profit sector. For this work, recipients do not receive a paycheck, benefits, sick time, or Social Security. Rather, they must work for their public assistance grant. The low benefit levels and increasing hours of work required will mean that, over time, depending on each state's benefit level, more and more women will be working for less than minimum wage. The increased hours will also mean that recipients will have less time to pursue additional education or searches for real jobs.

New York City, which started its workfare program prior to implementation of the federal law, has the most extensive workfare program in the nation. There, thousands of welfare recipients are cleaning the streets and picking up litter in the parks, while at the same time the number of regular city employees in these positions has been steadily reduced. The incentive to use welfare recipients, who are paid from federal funds, rather than to hire workers who are often eligible for union-negotiated higher wages and fringe benefits, will be great. Consequently, states will have little incentive to provide the supports that will enable this compulsory workforce to move into real jobs. After 2 years, when workfare participants reach the point where they must have real jobs, those who do not will be cut off from assistance.

With a time limit for receipt of welfare, what will these women do? Many will decide to return to their husbands or boyfriends or try to find other men to support them and their children. In fact, conservative commentators touting "family values" have made marriage an explicit goal of welfare reform. They are concerned that welfare has encouraged single-parent families and seem to be more concerned with maintaining two-parent families than with ensuring safe families. In Minnesota, prior to the new federal welfare law, a waiver was granted so that the state could provide incentives for welfare recipients to marry. These promarriage values have been codified in the PRA itself. Among the purposes of the PRA are to "(2) end the dependence of needy parents on government benefits by promoting job preparation, work, and marriage;" and "(4) encourage the formation and maintenance of two-parent families" (Personal Responsibility and Work Opportunity Reconciliation Act of 1996, 110 Stat. 2105, 2113).

The New Welfare Law and Abused Women

As onerous as the provisions of the PRA are for all women needing public assistance, it has even more profound implications for victims of family violence. Under the former welfare provisions, Aid to Families With Dependent Children (AFDC), which the Temporary Assistance to Needy Families (TANF) provisions in the PRA replaced, it was difficult enough for a woman to make a choice to leave her abuser when it meant applying for welfare. Under these new, more stringent provisions, women are likely to be even more reluctant to leave. For women who have already left violent, abusive relationships, the lifetime limit and work rules may prove lethal. In effect, the government is encouraging women to stay or return to their abusers or to find other men—any men who can provide material support—in order to feed their families. For these women, and even for those who were not previously abused, financial desperation may cloud their judgment so that they may rush into new relationships with men who will be abusive to them or their children.

What will be the options for the woman who is no longer eligible for welfare, who cannot support herself and her children, and does not find a man to provide for her? She and her children may become homeless, or she may be driven to illegal activities to provide for her children. If she cannot provide for them, she may lose custody because of neglect or abandonment.

Education

Abused women are at least as likely to have the same low educational level as the average welfare recipient. To become financially independent, she may need not only time to complete her high school education or equivalency but also further education and training in order to compete for a job that will pay a living wage and provide some security. High school graduates earn more than nongraduates, and women with even 2-year associate's degrees earn 65% more than women with high school diplomas (Kates, n.d.; U.S. Department of Education, 1994).[3] Further education or job training to enable women to become financially independent may take more than the 2 years of public assistance before a real job is required. Because under the new law a recipient must still work a minimum of 20 hours each week in workfare, she may only be able to manage one or two courses each semester even if she is highly motivated. That will mean a longer time to complete an education that enables her to support her family at a living wage.

Low Self-Esteem and
Post-Traumatic Stress Disorder

For some women, achieving financial independence will not be as clear-cut as just obtaining the needed education or training. Women who have experienced abuse over time are likely to have lowered self-esteem. If the one person a woman is close to is her abuser who repeatedly tells her she is stupid, fat, ugly, or incompetent, after a while she begins to believe these images of herself. This is especially true when, as is the frequent pattern, a woman has been isolated from friends and family who might see her differently. She may have lost confidence in her own abilities and her own judgment. That she has left the situation, has obtained public assistance, and is striking out on her own takes great fortitude. But a poor interview, a low test grade, or a critical comment from a supervisor may be enough for her to lose her faith in herself, at least for a time. If she loses her job, does not show up for an appointment, fails to return to a workfare site, or drops out of a training program, she can be sanctioned and lose some or all of her assistance. As Boyer documents in Chapter 10, women who had been sexually abused as children and who subsequently turned to public assistance as adults because of teenage pregnancy may have particular difficulties in maintaining employment.

Counselors working with victims of abuse have documented that many suffer from post-traumatic stress disorder (PTSD), a recognized mental disorder (American Psychological Association [APA], 1994, pp. 424-429). This syndrome was first noticed by therapists working with veterans of the Vietnam War who exhibited a range of symptoms months or years after their grueling frontline experiences. Nightmares, overreactions, flashbacks, depression, escape into substance abuse, and depression are some symptoms of the disorder (APA, 1994, pp. 424-429). Women surviving partner abuse were found to exhibit these same symptoms. And why not? They have also been in a battle zone, their lives, too, have been in danger—and for many, for a lot longer than the war veteran.

PTSD is not limited to victims of partner abuse. Women who suffered extreme physical or sexual abuse as children may also exhibit these symptoms if they have not been treated. Moreover, many victims of domestic violence were also victims of abuse as children; thus, it is even harder for them to overcome their feelings of worthlessness and low self-esteem (Beitchman et al., 1992). Simply forcing women to "get it together" by harsh cut-off provisions will not motivate them to change.

Not all women escaping abusive situations exhibit PTSD. Some overcome the symptoms soon after the abuse stops. For others, however, the symptoms become chronic. Shelter workers have found that it takes the battered woman an average of seven attempts to finally leave her batterer (Rawlings, 1997). How many psychic, as well as physical, traumas has she accumulated during that time? For these women, not only is the 5-year (or less) lifetime limit problematic, but of more immediate concern is the requirement to participate in workfare within a mere 2 months of initial receipt of assistance and then to obtain a job within 2 years.

Sabotage of Work Efforts

Some women who are trying to become financially independent of welfare are sabotaged by the men in their lives, as documented by Raphael in Chapter 3. The men may do it subtly, by convincing the women of their lack of ability, by provoking conflict before an important test or interview, or more blatantly by beating, harassing, or stalking them at their places of work. An abuser's behavior may cause an employer to let the woman go in order to avoid trouble in the workplace and to protect the safety of others.

Effect on Children

Another obstacle that may prevent abused women from meeting the time limits in the PRA is the effect on their children. For all women on public assistance, finding accessible and quality child care is an issue. Although federal and many state laws have increased the funding provided for child care, it is questionable whether the increase will be sufficient for the escalating number of women now being forced to work. "Despite this new money, if all states meet their welfare work targets CBO [Congressional Budget Office] projects that child care funding falls $1.4 billion short of the need for welfare families" (Children's Defense Fund, 1996, p. 15).

For the abused woman, however, there is a complicating factor. Children who witness abuse are affected by it (Pagelow, 1981). Whether they are actually in the same room, hear the shouting from their bedroom, or see the bruises on their mother the next morning, they are affected. In one focus group I ran, a woman who had just left an abusive marriage said, "My children need me at home to love them and cuddle them. I can't go to work now." In another, a woman remarked that finding child care for her children was difficult. As a result of the abuse and turmoil in the family, the children were acting out—in her words, "off the wall." Their behavior was uncontrollable in the child care center, which refused to keep them in care. Without child care, their mother lost her job.

Child Support

The PRA sets stringent requirements for the collection of child support payments to reimburse states for funds expended on public assistance. As Roberts discusses in Chapter 5, the effects of requiring a mother to report on the paternity and whereabouts of the absent, abusive father can put her and her children in jeopardy. Rather than punish the fathers, who are difficult to find or may be able to hide their assets, the law punishes the mothers by withholding or reducing payments if they do not cooperate. The non-cooperating fathers are held innocent until proved guilty through the court process; the mother who is dependent on public assistance is judged to be uncooperative and does not have the same recourse. She is judged guilty unless she can prove her innocence through an appeal process. But the federal government no longer even requires states to provide for "fair hear-ing" appeals.

Current law, as discussed in Chapter 5, provides for a waiver from child support reporting in cases of family violence, but this has been underused. Moreover, the new Family Violence Option for the states provides for the possibility of a waiver from child support reporting by domestic violence victims if doing so would put them at further risk. Ironically, many abused women do not want waivers; they want the children's fathers to be held responsible and are often angry with the child support enforcement authorities for not being more aggres-sive in finding them and demanding payment or punishing them if they refuse to pay.

Residency Requirement

One option the PRA leaves for states to choose is a residency requirement. This gives states the right to adopt different levels of financial assistance or a waiting period for public assistance applicants moving from another state. Some states have opted for a residency requirement. In New York, this entails providing a grant equal to the state from which the woman moved for the first year, if this amount is less than New York's (State of New York, 1997, Sect. 349A, pp. 112-113). Residency provisions may be unconstitutional, and some cases are already pending. Similar legislation in the past was struck by the Supreme Court as interfering with the right to travel and equal treatment provisions of the Constitution.

As depicted by Davis in Chapter 2, such residency requirements may have the chilling effect of discouraging a woman from fleeing from a violent abuser, at risk to her and her children's lives. Fleeing to another state where her abuser cannot find her may be her only chance for safety. If she does move and if her assistance level is below subsistence, she may be forced to either return to her original state— and thus endanger herself and her family—or try to find another man to help support her.

The Wellstone-Murray Family Violence Amendment

As discussed in Chapter 1, Senators Paul Wellstone and Patti Murray sponsored an amendment to the Personal Responsibility Act known as the Family Violence Amendment. In the original legislation passed by the Senate, the amendment would have been a requirement, but in conference a compromise was reached with the House and it emerged in the final bill as an option for states to adopt if they choose.

Provisions of the Amendment

The provisions of the amendment include (a) screening of applicants with a history of domestic violence while maintaining confidentiality, (b) referring such identified individuals to counseling and supportive services, and (c) making good cause waivers for such program requirements as time limits, residency requirements, child support cooperation requirements, family cap provisions, or any other requirements that "would make it more difficult for individuals receiving assistance . . . to escape domestic violence, to unfairly penalize such individuals . . ., or individuals who are at risk for further domestic violence (Personal Responsibility and Work Opportunity Reconciliation Act of 1996, Section 103, Subsection 402 [a][7]).[4] Currently, 28 states have chosen to adopt the Family Violence Option and are in various stages of proceduralizing and implementing it (NOW Legal Defense and Education Fund, 1997).

The amendment was constructed to address the issues that have been discussed throughout this volume. For the first time, a federal policy recognizes that women applying for welfare may be victims of domestic violence. In recognition of the difficulties and potential dangers faced by such victims, it provides exceptions from some of the requirements of the welfare law. Among these are the work provisions and the 5-year limit that would be difficult to achieve, thus unfairly penalizing such women, and the residency and child support reporting requirements, which could further endanger them.

Objections to the Family Violence Option

Objections to adopting the option have come from two quarters: from state administrators responsible for its implementation and, ironically, from those in the battered women's movement.

Too Few or Too Many

The very research that documented the need for the amendment is now being used as a reason not to adopt it. The frequency data gathered in such disparate areas as Washington, Massachusetts, New York City, and elsewhere (Allard, Colten, Albelda, & Cosenza, 1997; Kenney & Brown, 1997; Raphael & Tolman, 1997; Washington State Institute for Public Policy, 1993) found that between 30% and 80% of women receiving AFDC had a past or current experience with domestic violence and that over 30% of battered women with police incident reports used public assistance (Brandwein, 1997). Once the extent of the problem was recognized, it could be addressed in federal legislation.

Now, however, administrators responsible for implementing welfare reform are afraid that too many women will be eligible for the waiver. Not only would it put pressure on available services, but they fear they could lose federal funds. The PRA allows states to waive up to 20% of their caseload from the 5-year lifetime limit for "good cause." A large group of people already need good cause waivers because of health or mental health problems unrelated to domestic violence. State administrators fear that, with all these additionally identified victims of domestic violence, the 20% maximum would be exceeded, which could entail federal financial penalties known as "sanctions."

Senators Wellstone and Murray offered Amendment 480 to the PRA to clarify that their intent of the legislation was to provide waivers for these women above and beyond the 20%. The Department of Health and Human Services (DHHS), however, recently issued regulations that would merely provide states with the ability to seek individual exceptions for cause for domestic violence exemptions that bring a state above the 20% maximum (DHHS, 1997a). This will have the effect of discouraging waivers because the regulations will require increased record keeping and postaudits. Because states cannot be assured that the waivers they issue will be acceptable to federal auditors, they risk losing federal funds if their waivers are not approved by an after-the-fact review by the DHHS. Both pressures for additional services and the risk of exceeding their waiver quota could increase state budgets at a time of general clamor for reducing taxes.

From Lazy to Crazy?

The position of administrators who are sensitive to political pressures and taxpayers' concerns is perhaps more easily understandable than the criticisms of the Family Violence Option from some of those providing services to battered women. One source of criticism emanates from a class distinction. The battered women's movement has been successful in bringing the problem of family violence to the fore in the nation's consciousness by portraying it, accurately, as a phenomenon that cuts across race, ethnicity, religion, and education and income levels. Because the public perceives family violence as a problem that can—and does—happen to their neighbors, their relatives, or even themselves, there is now broad public support for efforts to address and combat it.

Acknowledgment of the perception that victims of domestic violence are now seen sympathetically led to advocates in the welfare reform battle to link domestic violence with welfare. Some believe that linking the two issues might make the public more sympathetic to the plight of welfare recipients. Those working in the battered women's movement, however, fear that it could have the opposite effect: that the negative stereotypes of welfare recipients would attach to all domestic violence victims, who would once again be seen as the "other," undeserving of our help and sympathy.

Related to this is the fear that as more welfare recipients are identified as having been victims of domestic violence and are referred for services, service providers' resources will be overwhelmed. Already, most services are understaffed and oversubscribed. If additional funds are not made available for service expansion, how will providers serve all those identified? And who will receive priority for services? Will a requirement to serve those welfare clients identified as domestic violence victims drive out other clients—either because of inadequate resources to serve both or because of stereotypes of welfare clients held by nonwelfare clients?

Yet another aspect of the negative response to the Family Violence Option on the part of some service providers, and some welfare clients as well, is that it will simply lead to further stigmatization and marginalization. Some women who have been victims of domestic violence fear that, by choosing the waiver, they will be denied access to education, training, and jobs so that they can improve their lives.

Rather than enabling them to receive supportive services, they fear that such identification will simply consign them to the slag heap of receiving nothing because resources for supportive services and placements are likely to be limited.[5] They do not wish to remain in the netherworld of welfare dependency indefinitely; they want help to be able to support themselves. They fear that, by being identified in the public record as victims of domestic violence, they will be considered mentally impaired and less competent. As one woman said, "Before, the stereotype was that women on welfare were all lazy, now the stereotype will be that they're crazy—which is worse?"

Implementation of the Family Violence Option

Implementation of the Family Violence Option, like implementation of every law, depends on the understanding and commitment of those responsible for implementation. Administrators responsible for public assistance often have little understanding of the phenomenon of family violence. In many states, the option was adopted as a result of advocacy and public pressure on lawmakers. Lawmakers, who hear directly from constituents, may be more sympathetic to the issues of domestic violence than middle-level managers, who are often inured in a bureaucratic mind-set of waiting for regulations and procedures to come down from above. Top administrators of public assistance are often politically appointed and held accountable for curbing costs. Rather than service to clients as their first priority, they are responsible, first, not to exceed their budgets and to hold the caseload down.

For many administrators of public assistance programs, the Family Violence Option will be seen as just one more complicating factor that will put pressure on an already inadequate staff. Screening and assessment will require staff time, and not all states adopting the option included increases to departmental budgets for additional staff to implement it.

Screening

The first requirement of the option is confidential screening. How this screening will occur is a topic of discussion around the country.

In my focus groups with abused women who are or have been on welfare, I heard their concerns about this process. "I'm not going to tell a welfare worker . . . they'd be the last one I'd tell." They were apprehensive about disclosing these painful and highly personal issues with workers they perceived as being overburdened and busy at best, and uncaring and judgmental at worst. They distrusted the system and had little faith that disclosing would really help them or that confidentiality would be protected.

The success of the Family Violence Option is directly dependent on how and by whom the screening is done. Will it be done by the overworked eligibility workers? If so, will they receive training in how to ask questions? Will it be contracted out to family violence specialists? Will it be done on the first visit or subsequently, after a trusting relationship is developed that makes disclosure of sensitive issues more likely? Will it be done, as proposed by New York, on a form as part of a large application package? Screening in this way or by eligibility workers at the initial face-to-face interview almost guarantees very low numbers of victim self-identification. Perhaps this is, if not the latent purpose, then the unintended consequence of such methods: The fewer women identified as domestic violence victims, the less pressure on overburdened staff, the lower the cost for services, and the fewer waivers needed and the less possibility of federal sanctions.

An additional chilling effect on disclosure of domestic violence is the possibility, being considered in some states, of tying disclosure of domestic violence to child abuse reporting. It is finally being recognized that, in many families where one form of abuse is present, so is the other (Bowker, Arbitell, & Ferron, 1988; Stark & Flitcraft, 1985). Moreover, growing evidence suggests that the very witnessing of domestic violence between adults in the home is harmful to children and can be considered a form of emotional abuse (Pagelow, 1981). For these reasons, New York officials have added an informed consent statement in their screening document. This informs applicants for public assistance that their disclosure may prompt a child protective services investigation. Under the guise of protecting children, they are, in effect, warning applicants that if they identify themselves as victims of domestic violence, they might risk losing custody of their children. The likely outcome of such a procedure may have a chilling effect on use of the Family Violence Option.[6]

Assessment and Referral to Services

Once the screening has identified victims of abuse, the next step is an assessment process to determine what counseling or other services are needed and whether any waivers are necessary for the individual client. Once again, the question is, Who will do the assessments and how they will be done? In the New York enabling legislation, a "family violence liaison" is to be identified in each county. The person identified, most likely a member of the current staff, would receive training in domestic violence. It is unlikely that many local departments of social services would have on their staffs individuals with prior experience or expertise in this area or the financial ability to hire a new staffperson with such expertise.[7]

The role of the liaison, according to the statute (State of New York, 1997, p. 113), will be to document the accuracy of the domestic violence claim and to assess what services are needed. This combines an investigative function with helping and advocacy functions. The documentation process may convey a message to the woman that she is doubted; that once again, like in other encounters with public assistance staff, she is suspected of cheating. After this encounter, how will the liaison be able to engage the woman in honest communication about her needs and fears?

An alternative implementation model contracts out the assessment function to not-for-profit organizations already serving battered women. This alternative has already been implemented in Idaho and is being considered in New York and other states. It would seem preferable because, unfortunately, the image of the public assistance office is not that of helping and advocating, but of investigating and distrusting the client. Although ideally that image might be changed if more supportive and helpful services could be provided by the public agency, in the short term this is unlikely. Therefore, removing the function of assessment from the public assistance office and staff may lead to more open communication and honest appraisal by sympathetic and knowledgeable domestic violence counselors who perceive their role as advocates for their clients.

This strategy also has its drawbacks. One fear is the potential co-optation of the contract agency. Will the agency be under pressure from the public assistance department not to give too many waivers? Because waivers for domestic violence are not counted separately from the total 20% allowed, the agency doing the assessments will be put in the untenable position of advocating for waivers for their clients at the expense of others in need of waivers: clients of drug and alcohol, mental health, and vocational rehabilitation agencies. Once again, those in need will be pitted against each other for limited resources.

Will assessments made by the contract domestic violence agency be subject to review and denial by the public assistance department? Does a potential conflict of interest exist if the domestic violence agency recommends services that it provides? Because the law is so new, these are just conjectures now, but care needs to be taken in how the assessment process is implemented. Ideally, it will work best where there is close collaboration among the public assistance office, battered women's programs, mental health agencies, education and job-training programs, and child care facilities. Those doing the assessments should also identify unmet service needs in the community and work with others to advocate for additional resources. Care will need to be taken so that services presumed to help do not actually result in punishment.

Analysis and Policy Recommendations

Welfare, like domestic violence, is a gender issue. Until very recently, abused women, like women on welfare, were blamed for their situations, for "getting themselves into trouble," and were stereotyped negatively. Welfare recipients are in double jeopardy; not only are they women, but they also are poor. Very often, they are also women of color, which puts them in triple jeopardy.

Too frequently, after a law is finally passed to help these women, it can become so distorted that they are once again being blamed and, in effect, punished for their situation. Child support enforcement legislation is one example of this phenomenon. Ostensibly passed so that noncustodial fathers would be made to share the responsibility of supporting their children, the 1988 federal Family Support Act tightened support requirements, amounts, and reporting responsibility. It had the effect, however, of holding the mothers seeking public assistance responsible for reporting, rather than holding the fathers responsible for payment. A father may still not be found nor his income proven, but the woman is in a position to be punished if she fails to report, whereas he is rarely punished for failure to pay support.

Similarly, in a child abuse situation where the mother is not the abuser, she is still held responsible for protecting the child. The abuser may just leave the home and is seldom arraigned or convicted in court for his abuse or neglect (Schwartzberg, 1992; Spengel, 1993). If, however, she is unable to protect the child from him or to demonstrate adequate supervision, she can lose custody of her child. The abuser who caused the trauma to the child is rarely punished. Rather than helping the mother protect her child against the abuser, the child protective system punishes her with the threat of the loss of her child.

A similar pattern may be emerging with the implementation of the Family Violence Option. Designed as a way to help, support, and protect welfare recipients who have been victims of domestic violence, it is in danger of being perverted into another exercise in blaming the victim.

The example described earlier, of warning women in their screening document that if they identify themselves as victims of domestic violence they may open themselves to a child protective services investigation, is a case in point. Women are not warned that if they report domestic violence incidents to the police, they may be subject to a child protective services investigation. If they were warned, few would report. Whether intended or not, such a statement would have the effect of stifling reporting and hence the opportunity to receive needed services and waivers from welfare requirements or of subjecting these women to the risk of the ultimate punishment for most mothers: the risk of losing their children.

In some states, a woman who has self-identified as a domestic violence victim may be required to develop a "safety plan" with her worker. This in itself is not problematic. Such plans, that elucidate how women will escape abusive situations or avoid their harassers, are often developed by women and their counselors or shelter workers. The plans are designed to give them some structure and empower them. They may or may not follow their plans, depending on the situation and their own fortitude. If these state procedures are implemented, however, women on welfare who violate their own safety plans or who have obtained waivers and do not follow their service plans could be sanctioned and lose their benefits. Once again, the abused woman on welfare is "punished." The PRA also targets unwed pregnant teenagers and sets out specific strictures and requirements for their receipt of assistance, rather than providing victims of childhood sexual abuse the help to recover from this trauma and thus reduce the likelihood of early pregnancies.

In these examples, not only is the woman on welfare punished rather than her male abuser, but she is also treated differently from the domestic violence victim or the pregnant teenager who is not receiving welfare.

Short-Term Strategies

States that have not yet adopted the Family Violence Option should be encouraged to do so. It is still a means for recognizing the unique difficulties faced by victims of abuse and provides the potential for protecting them from harmful effects of the new welfare legislation. In those states that have adopted it, advocates for both the poor and the victims of domestic violence will need to review proposed state plans carefully for its implementation.

It is necessary for screening and assessment to be done by trained, sensitive personnel, in face-to-face interviews, preferably in more than one meeting. This will require adequate funding for training and hiring or contracting with qualified personnel. It may also be necessary to augment available community services such as counseling, legal services, transitional housing, and child care. Appropriate child care programs and personnel will be needed for children suffering the effects of having witnessed abuse. Coordination and collaboration among agencies providing services are necessary in an ongoing, structured way in each community. Some communities already have domestic violence councils; those providing public assistance and workfare placements must be included in these bodies.

More attention must be given to the abusers. Domestic violence has finally been redefined as a criminal justice issue. The 1994 federal Violence Against Women Act has been a major force in this change. A recent amendment to the unemployment insurance laws now enables a woman who loses her job because of harassment to collect unemployment insurance. Tougher criminal laws and their enforcement for harassment and stalking, at the workplace as well as at home, may be necessary. With such enforcement in place, employers could then be prohibited from firing women who are being harassed at work.

Real Reform: Longer-Term Strategies and Universal Approaches to Change

As President Clinton said when he first introduced his ill-fated welfare bill, welfare cannot simply be changed by changing the welfare system. We must look beyond the immediate adjustments to the existing welfare laws and address the larger issues that necessitate the need for welfare, for both abused women and other poor women.

Adequate Jobs and Income

In the president's proposed welfare plan, like the one adopted, welfare recipients would also have been required to work after 2 years. If, however, recipients were not able to find work after a good faith effort, the government would have guaranteed them subsidized employment. If we expect people to work and if jobs are not available, the government must, in effect, become the employer of last resort. Despite optimistic reports of falling unemployment rates and a national jobless rate of under 5%, in December 1997 the official unemployment rate in New York City was over 9%. This figure does not include those working part time because they cannot find full-time employment or discouraged workers who are no longer actively seeking employment. A recent report by the Milton Eisenhower Foundation, "The Millennium Breach," reports that the jobless rate is over 30% for young people in some inner-city communities (Associated Press, 1998, p. A25).

Welfare and poverty, it must be remembered, are gender related. Women working full time, full year still earn only about 70% of what men earn. Women with a college education earn only slightly more than men with a high school education (U.S. Department of Education, 1994).[8] Because women, particularly those with less education, tend to work for lower wages and in temporary jobs, they are less likely to be covered by unemployment insurance when they lose employment. Because gender-related job inequities have not been addressed, welfare has become the safety net for women. Now even this meager safety net can no longer be assured.

If work were available at a living wage, fewer women would need to turn to the welfare system. Passage of equitable job laws, assuring equal pay for work with similar job requirements, duties and responsibilities would help address the wage gap for women. A living wage could be assured by tying the minimum wage to the cost of living and adjusting it annually, as is now done for Social Security. By that one policy change, adjusting Social Security benefits for those over age 65 to the cost of living, the number of poor elderly in the United States was dramatically reduced. According to data from population reports of the U.S. Bureau of the Census for 1966 through 1995, the elderly went from being the demographic group with the highest poverty rate before those changes to being the group with the lowest poverty rate (Sturiale, 1997, p. 27).

Health Coverage

Another means of reducing the numbers of people needing welfare would be the adoption of guaranteed health benefits for all. In some states, families can receive Medicaid only if they are also receiving public assistance. Women leaving welfare often obtain jobs in the secondary labor market with no health coverage. If they or their children become ill, they may be forced to quit their jobs and seek public assistance to obtain medical coverage. Mothers who have chronic health problems or who have children with such problems may turn to welfare because the jobs they can get do not provide health coverage or the cost to the employee is prohibitive. Women who have been domestic violence victims are more likely to suffer from chronic physical ailments. If their children have been abused, they too may have chronic health problems. President Clinton addressed health reform prior to welfare reform in his first term because he understood that, by providing universal health coverage, it would be easier to address what would then be a smaller welfare population.[9]

Child Care

Accessible, affordable, quality child care is a necessity not only for the welfare recipient required to work but for all working parents. As of this writing, the president has proposed billions of dollars for additional child care. Currently, welfare recipients are pitted against the working poor for limited child care subsidies and available slots. It is a case of "musical chairs," as poor working mothers who cannot afford child care are forced to apply for public assistance. While on public assistance, child care is provided to those working or in workfare placements, but once they leave the rolls, they may once again be unable to find affordable, accessible care.

A recent incident of an infant who died in the care of an au pair hit a sensitive nerve with the millions of families in which the mothers of infants need to be employed. Child development studies indicate that the mental stimulation provided during the first 3 years of life are essential to children's mental development. Yet, the PRA requires mothers with children over the age of 1 to be employed or in workfare placements and gives states the option to require employment from women with infants only 3 months old. It also allows, for the first time, noncertified, uninspected, "informal" child care arrangements for welfare recipients. In New York City, this has already caused some women to be pressured to accept lower-cost, informal child care instead of Head Start or other quality, educational child care.[10] Unless we as a society are prepared to invest in stimulating, educational environments for poor children, we will ensure the continuation and exacerbation of inequality in the next generation.

Educational Opportunities

Inequities in education, not just at the infant and preschool levels but in primary and secondary education, must be addressed (Kozol, 1991). Why are so many high school graduates functionally illiterate? Reliance on local property taxes to fund school districts institutionalizes differences between the middle class and the poor. Children in poor districts receive poorer educations and cannot compete for available jobs. Women who have been victims of domestic violence who leave their abusers often experience downward mobility and must move their families to lower-cost housing with inferior schools.

Access to free or affordable higher education to all who can benefit from it should be a right. When the City University system in New York was free, it educated several generations of children of immigrants and the poor, many of whom went on to excel in their fields. To discourage welfare recipients from going to college (when they are motivated to do so) by disallowing education as a work activity and simultaneously increasing tuition at public institutions of higher learning creates a permanent underclass in our society. Such policies deny the American dream of opportunity and upward mobility to all who are willing to work for it. Women who have more education are less likely to be trapped in violent relationships. They are also less likely to stay on welfare (Kates, n.d.). They have the skills and the abilities to support themselves without having to resort to welfare.

Affordable Housing

The lack of affordable housing is a major reason that women stay or return to abusers. Those who escape to a battered women's shelter can stay only a short time, usually a maximum of 30 to 60 days. After that, they must face homelessness or return to their abusers unless they have extended family to take them in. Even those arrangements are often precarious and short-lived (Lazere, Dolbeare, Leonard, & Zigas, 1991).

Housing costs have escalated in many city and suburban areas around the nation. Even those women who go on welfare find that they cannot afford to pay their rent and still pay for other necessities. Decent, affordable housing does not mean the housing projects of generations past that concentrated the very poor in one place where they were ignored by municipal services and were vulnerable to criminal elements who preyed upon them. Section 8, a federal program that subsidizes private housing, is terribly underfunded. In some communities, the waiting list for a Section 8 certificate is 2 or 3 years; in others, the lists have been closed. Even women who have certificates have found they could not locate appropriate dwellings that would accept their certificates. More affordable rental housing needs to be constructed, expanding the supply and reducing costs by lowering the demand for the scarce units currently available. If laws economically integrated rental housing and prevented communities from passing prohibitive zoning to exclude rental units, abused women would no longer be forced to choose between a safe home and a safe community.

Conclusion

All of these recommendations address the needs of the working poor and the nonpoor, as well as those on welfare. Services designed just for the poor result in poor services. Unless a broad spectrum of taxpayers use a service, the public will not support it. Services targeted for welfare recipients are likely to be inferior and vulnerable to cuts, if they are passed at all. Even if they are passed, they tend to be administered punitively. Housing, education, health care, and child care are universal needs. If we rely on the private, market system for meeting these needs, only those with high incomes will be able to afford them. Not only will the rest of the population suffer, but we will all suffer if these people are unable to contribute to the society.

The idea of government-supported services is not popular today, but it is time to reverse the trend of privatization whereby each person and family is responsible only for themselves. We have finally learned that family violence is not a private issue, but a societal concern. We are interdependent, and as a nation and a community we need to provide collectively that which we cannot provide individually. The scourge of family violence is universal in our society. Its solutions must be so as well.

Notes

1. *Secondary labor market* is a term used in economics referring to jobs that require usually unskilled labor and little education. They generally provide no fringe benefits and often offer only part-time or temporary work with no job security.

2. The U.S. Department of Health and Human Services has established poverty guidelines for more than 30 years, based on a minimum food budget and adjusted each year for cost of living changes. In 1997, the poverty guidelines in the 48 contiguous states were $13,330 for a family of three, $16,050 for a family of four, and slightly higher in Alaska and Hawaii.

3. According to the U.S. Department of Education's *Digest of Education Statistics* (1994, p. 399), women working full-time without a high school education can expect to earn $14,613 annually; those with a high school degree, an average of $19,462; and those with a college degree, $30,394. Rationally, it would appear that encouraging education is the best way to ensure that women could support their families without relying on public assistance, yet the new law does not include education as counting toward the 20-hour work requirement.

4. The following is the complete text of the Family Violence Amendment found in Section 103—Block Grants to States—Subsection 402(a)(7) of the Personal Responsibility and Work Opportunity Reconciliation Act of 1996:

OPTIONAL CERTIFICATION OF STANDARDS AND PROCEDURES TO ENSURE THAT THE STATE WILL SCREEN FOR AND IDENTIFY DO-MESTIC VIOLENCE (i) screen and identify individuals receiving assistance under this part with a history of domestic violence while maintaining the confidentiality of such individuals; (ii) refer such individuals to counseling and support services; and (iii) waive, pursuant to a determination of good cause, other program requirements, such as time limits (for as long as necessary) for individuals receiving assistance, residency requirements, child support cooperation requirements and family cap provisions, in cases where compliance with such requirements would make it more difficult for individuals receiving assistance under this part to escape domestic violence or unfairly penalize such individuals who are or have been victimized by such violence, or individuals who are at risk of further domestic violence.

(B) DOMESTIC VIOLENCE DEFINED—For purposes of this paragraph, the term "domestic violence" has the same meaning as the term "battered or subject to extreme cruelty" as defined in section 408(a)(7)(C)(iii).

* *

Subsec. 408(a)(7)(C)(iii)—Battered or Subject to Extreme Cruelty Defied: . . . an individual has been battered or subjected to extreme cruelty if the individual has been subjected to (I) physical acts that resulted in, or threatened to result in, physical injury to the individual; (II) sexual abuse; (III) sexual activity involving a dependent child; (IV) being forced as the caretaker relative of a dependent child to engage in nonconsensual sexual acts or activities; (V) threats of, or attempts at, physical or sexual abuse; (VI) mental abuse or (VII) neglect or deprivation of medical care.

5. Those expressing this concern may not understand that, under the new welfare law, higher education will no longer be available, and even vocational training opportunities will be very limited. A total of 1 year is allowable but only for a maximum of 20% of the caseload, including teenagers without high school degrees, who must be in a high school or equivalency program. If they consider a workfare placement a positive opportunity, they may be correct as only 25% to 50% of the caseload will be required to participate, and those identified as victims of domestic violence may be excluded. The waiver is not automatic, however, but is only allowed when an assessment determines that such placement would jeopardize or further penalize the woman.

6. We have just learned that, in one community on Long Island, New York, where screening with this statement is being targeted, predictably only 17 women out of more than 500 who applied for public assistance in early 1998 identified themselves as past or current victims of domestic violence. This is less than 5%, compared with the McCormack Institute's figures of over one third in a representative sample of public assistance applicants (Allard et al., 1997).

7. Recently promulgated rules of the New York State Office of Temporary and Disability Assistance list the minimum job qualifications for domestic violence liaison as:
   (a) be a caseworker, or
       (1) possess a bachelor's degree, or
       (2) have one year of domestic violence advocacy or domestic violence counseling experience with an approved domestic violence program, or
       (3) have two years of relevant advocacy or domestic counseling experience; and
   (b) complete a course of training for domestic violence liaisons sponsored by the Office of Temporary and Disability Assistance; and
   (c) possess good communication, listening and assessment skills and the ability to work positively in a team setting. (NYS Register, 1998, June 24, p. 33)

8. In 1994, a woman with a college education working full time earned an average annual wage of $30,394, compared with a man with a high school education's wage of $27,357. A woman with a high school education also working full time could expect to earn only $19,462 (U.S. Department of Education, 1994, p. 399).

9. Senator Paul Wellstone recently offered an amendment to a bill reauthorizing the Higher Education Act which would add postsecondary education as an eligible work activity for TANF recipients and extend to 24 months (from 12) the length of time postsecondary and vocational education could count as work.

10. At a hearing before a New York State Assembly joint committee considering welfare reform on January 23, 1997, a recipient of public assistance in New York City testified that her worker pressured her to remove her child from Head Start and to substitute baby-sitting by a neighbor (informal care) because it would be less expensive.

References

Allard, M. A., Colten, M. E., Albelda, R., & Cosenza, C. (1997). *In harm's way? Domestic violence, AFDC receipt, and welfare reform in Massachusetts.* Boston: University of Massachusetts, McCormack Institute, Center for Survey Research.

American Psychological Association (APA). (1994). *Desk reference to the diagnostic criteria from DSM-IV* (4th ed.). Washington, DC: Author.

Associated Press. (1998, March 1). Report: Race gap widening in U.S. *Newsday,* p. A25.

Bane, M. J., & Ellwood, D. (1983). *The dynamics of dependency: The roots to self-sufficiency.* Unpublished manuscript prepared for U.S. Department of Health and Human Services, Washington, DC.

Beitchman, J., et al. (1992). A review of the long-term effects of child sexual abuse. *Journal of Child Abuse and Neglect, 16,* 110-118.

Bowker, L. H., Arbitell, M., & Ferron, J. R. (1988). On the relationship between wife beating and child abuse. In K. Yllo & M. Bograd (Eds.), *Feminist perspectives on wife abuse* (pp. 158-174). Newbury Park, CA: Sage.

Brandwein, R. (1997, May) *Links between family violence and welfare reform: The Utah experience and national implications.* Paper presented at the Fifth International Conference on Family Violence, Durham, NH.

Children's Defense Fund. (1996). *Summary of legislation affecting children in 1996.* Washington, DC: Author.

Ellwood, D. (1988). *Poor support: Poverty in the American family.* New York: Basic Books.

Kates, E. (n.d.). *Getting smart about welfare.* Washington, DC: Center for Women's Policy Studies.

Kenney, C., & Brown, K. (1997). *Report from the front lines: The impact of violence on poor women.* New York: NOW Legal Defense and Education Fund.

Kozol, J. (1991). *Savage inequalities.* New York: Crown.

Lazere, E., Dolbeare, C., Leonard, P., & Zigas, B. (1991). *A place to call home: The low-income housing crisis continues.* Washington, DC: Center on Budget and Policy Priorities and Low-Income Housing Information Services.

NOW Legal Defense and Education Fund. (1997). *Summary of state activity regarding family violence provisions in their state welfare plans.* Washington, DC: Author.

Pagelow, M. D. (1981). Effects of domestic violence on children and their consequence for custody and visitation agreements. *Mediation Quarterly, 7*(4), 347-363.

Personal Responsibility and Work Opportunity Reconciliation Act of 1996, Pub. L. 104-193, 110 Stat. 2105 (August 22, 1996).

Raphael, J., & Tolman, R. (1997). *Trapped by poverty/Trapped by abuse.* Chicago: Taylor Institute.

Rawlings, G. (1997, October 16). Guest lecture at Graduate Seminar on Family Violence, State University of New York at Stony Brook, School of Social Welfare.

Ruggles, P. (1989). Welfare dependency and its causes: Determinants of the duration of welfare spells. *Survey of Income and Program Participation* (Working Papers #8908).

Schwartzberg, R. (1992). *Does the court system "work" for sexually abused children?* Unpublished master's thesis, State University of New York at Stony Brook, School of Social Welfare.

Shea, M. (1992). *Characteristics of recipients and the dynamics of program participation, 1987-1988.* Washington, DC: U.S. Bureau of the Census.

Spalter-Roth, R., Hartmann, H., & Andrews, L. (1992). *Combining work and welfare: An alternative antipoverty program.* Washington, DC: Institute for Women's Policy Research.

Spengel, L. (1993). *What happens to sexually abused children in Suffolk County?* Independent study, John Jay College, Department of Forensic Psychology, New York.

Stark, E., & Flitcraft, A. (1985). Women battering, child abuse, and social heredity: What is the relationship? In N. Johnson (Ed.), *Marital violence* (pp. 147-171). Boston: Routledge Kegan Paul.

State of New York. An Act to Amend . . . Education, Labor and Social Services Budget, S.5788, A.8678, 1997-98 Regular Session (1997, August 4), § 349A, pp. 112-113.

Sturiale, J. (1997). *Poverty and income trends: 1995.* Washington, DC: Center on Budget and Policy Priorities.

U.S. Department of Education. (1994). *Digest of education statistics.* Washington, DC: Government Printing Office.

U.S. Department of Health and Human Services (DHHS), Administration of Children and Families. (1997a). *HHS fact sheet: Work not welfare: Clinton administration issues new proposed welfare regulations.* Washington, DC: Author.

U.S. Department of Health and Human Services (DHHS). (1997b). *1997 poverty guidelines* [On-line]. Available: http://aspe.os.dhhs.gov/poverty/97poverty.htm.

Washington State Institute for Public Policy. (1993). *Family income study.* Olympia: Author.

Welfare law cuts hundreds off the rolls. (1997, November 3). *New York Times,* pp. A1, B5.

Author Index

Subject Index

About the Contributors

Melissa Arch-Walton is a survivor of domestic violence and was a recipient of public assistance for 5 years. She is currently completing her bachelor's degree with a double major in pre-law and sociology at Southhampton College, New York, where she serves as Interim Assistant Director of the Multicultural Program. She was recently hired by the Southhampton Town Justice Court as a Domestic Violence Advocate in the local hospital.

Annie Boone is a survivor of domestic violence and former recipient of public assistance. She is currently employed as a Community Organizer for JEDI Women (Justice, Economic Dignity, and Independence for Women) in Salt Lake City, Utah.

Debra Boyer is Affiliate Assistant Professor in the Women's Studies Department at the University of Washington and Research Associate at the Center for Health Training in Seattle. She holds a Ph.D. in cultural anthropology and has numerous publications on adolescent pregnancy and sexual abuse, youth homelessness, and female prostitution.

Ruth A. Brandwein is Professor and former Dean of the School of Social Welfare at the State University of New York at Stony Brook. She cofounded and for 6 years chaired the Suffolk County Task Force on Family Violence. She currently serves on the National Council on Violence Against Women. For 4 years, she held the position of Commissioner of the Suffolk County (NY) Department of Social Services. She occupied the Belle Spafford Endowed Chair in Women and Families at the University of Utah Graduate School of Social Work and is the incoming President of the New York State Chapter of the National Association of Social Workers. The author of numerous publications in the areas of violence against women, women and poverty, family policy, and other women's issues, she is frequently called on as a speaker and op-ed contributor on issues of women and welfare. She holds degrees from Brandeis University (Ph.D.), University of Washington (M.S.W.), and Brooklyn College (B.A.).

Martha F. Davis is Legal Director of the NOW Legal Defense and Education Fund in New York City. She holds degrees from the University of Chicago (J.D.), Oxford University (M.A., B.A.), and Harvard University (A.B.), and currently serves as Adjunct Assistant Professor at the New York University School of Law. She is the author of *Brutal Need: Lawyers and the Welfare Rights Movement, 1960-1973* and writes frequently on issues affecting low-income women.

Ginger Erickson is a survivor of domestic violence and a former recipient of public assistance.

Diana May Pearce founded and directed the Women in Poverty Project of the Wider Opportunities for Women program in Washington, D.C. Widely recognized for coining the phrase "feminization of poverty," she has written, given presentations, and testified before Congress repeatedly on issues of women's poverty, economic inequality, and welfare reform. She received a Ph.D from the University of Michigan, was Visiting Scholar at the Institute for Research on Women and Gender at Stanford University, and is currently on the faculty of the School of Social Work of the University of Washington.

Jody Raphael has served as Executive Director of the Chicago-based Taylor Institute since 1994. One of the first persons to establish the link between domestic violence and welfare receipt, she is the author of numerous articles and publications on the subject. Currently, she collaborates with the University of Michigan Research Development Center on Poverty, Risk, and Mental Health in the Project for Research on Welfare, Work, and Domestic Violence. She hold degrees from the University of Chicago (J.D.) and Bryn Mawr College (B.A.).

Paula Roberts has been Senior Staff Attorney at the Center for Law and Social Policy (CLASP) in Washington, D.C., for the past 15 years. The author of more than 25 law review articles on welfare reform and child support, her recent publications include *Ending Poverty as We Know It: The Case for Child Support Enforcement and Assurance* and *Child Support Cooperation Issues Under the Personal Responsibility And Work Opportunities Act of 1996.* She is a graduate of Smith College and Fordham University Law School.

Diane M. Stuart, M.S., is State Coordinator for the Utah Governor's Cabinet Council on Domestic Violence and Serves as Director for the Utah Domestic Violence Advisory Council. For 5 years, she was Director of a battered women's shelter in Logan, Utah, and served as State Specialist for the Division of Child and Family Services. She provided testimony for the U.S. Senate Field Hearing on the Violence Against Women Act of 1993.